Jesus
A Beginner's Guide

ONEWORLD BEGINNER'S GUIDES combine an original, inventive, and engaging approach with expert analysis on subjects ranging from art and history to religion and politics, and everything in–between. Innovative and affordable, books in the series are perfect for anyone curious about the way the world works and the big ideas of our time.

Jesus
A Beginner's Guide

Anthony Le Donne

ONEWORLD

A Oneworld Book

First published Oneworld Publications, 2018

ISBN 978-1-78607-144-6
eISBN 978-1-78607-145-3

Images 1–27 and 30 are courtesy of Wikimedia. Images: Incantation bowl ©
Marie-Lan Nguyen; Magdala Stone © Hanay; Jesus Boat © Travellers & Tinkers;
Sermon on the Mount © Yelkrokoyade; Moscophoros © Ricardo *André Frantz;
The Good Shepherd mosaic* © Petar Milošević; Christ Pantocrater mosaic © Dianelos
Georgoudis; Tim Tebow © Ed Clemente Photography; Homeless Jesus © Anthony
Le Donne. The publishers are grateful to Timothy Schmalz and Tony Frey for their
permission to use the images 32–3.

Typeset by Fakenham Prepress Solutions, Fakenham, Norfolk, NR21 8NL
Printed and bound in Great Britain by Clays Ltd, Elcograf S.p.A

Oneworld Publications Ltd
10 Bloomsbury Street
London WC1B 3SR
England

For my father, Gary,
who has an open mind
and an open heart.

Contents

Acknowledgements

My colleagues and students at United Theological Seminary contributed in many ways to this book. Class discussions, doctoral focus groups, and even passing conversations in the hallway planted seeds. Special gratitude is owed to my research assistants, Ayad Attia and James Mallory. Many conversations with Tom Dozeman helped me think through the topic of ritual purity. Justus Hunter pointed me to a few invaluable resources related to pre-modern Christian thought. Dr. Hunter also read through an early draft of the manuscript and improved it. I am also grateful for the collegiality and generosity of Chris Keith, Joan Taylor, and Shadi Doostdar who helped me revise portions of this book.

This book is dedicated to my father. The dedication page notes that he has an open mind and an open heart. I thought about his open mind often as I imagined him reading this book. Much of the ground covered in this book was new to me and (perhaps) will be new to many readers. My father is the type of person who embraces new ideas; his intellectual curiosity makes him the ideal "interior voice" for this project. As to his open heart, just ask anyone who knows him. I am blessed to count myself among them.

List of illustrations

Introduction: A guidebook for a circuitous way

In these pages you will meet the many faces of Jesus. You will meet the small day laborer with short hair, no beard, and missing teeth. You will meet the symbolic, sacrificial lamb of John's imagination. You will meet the god-man of early Christian disputes. You will meet the warlord of Viking poetry. You will meet the muse for artistic exploration. In short, you will meet Jesus incarnated and reincarnated over the past 2,000 years.

Where to begin? Shall we begin with Jesus the political preacher? Jesus the resurrected holy man? Jesus the bannered icon of the medieval crusades? Jesus the personal savior of almost three billion Christians worldwide? So great is the impact of Jesus that his legacy is many and manifold.

From the very first, Jesus wears various masks. Even if we only focus on Jesus in the Bible, we are confronted with multiple portraits. Early Christianity placed four stories of his life side by side: the gospels of Matthew, Mark, Luke, and John. Or should we – as many scholars have – attempt to mine the gospels for the earliest recorded sayings of Jesus? This might provide an interesting mosaic of Jesus's career as a preacher, but we are confronted again by the lack of a singular portrait.

Any robust study of Jesus must acknowledge the many impressions of his legacy. This is not to say that historians cannot nail down several facts about his life, public career, and ideas.

But these facts must always relate in some way to how Jesus was honored and distorted in retrospect. Jesus, both theologically and metaphorically, continues to be revitalized in the lives of those who remember him.

The book before you, therefore, is not just a reconstruction of Jesus's life. Neither is it just the history of an idea. This guide for beginners is divided into five parts, each important for understanding Jesus's life and legacy.

Chapter One focuses on Jesus, the man. Here I provide several windows into his life and public career. This is a sketch from first-century memories, commemorations, and analysis of his social context deriving from the first century CE.

Chapter Two focuses on Jesus in early literature. This section gives an impression of Jesus's initial and explosive impact. Here I showcase Matthew's Jesus, Paul's Jesus, John's Jesus, etc. These are literary portraits, but each relates to the "Jesus of history" in some way. These early witnesses have the capacity to illustrate something true about Jesus. At the same time, these portraits create something unique; each new portrait of Jesus is an invention that captures a stage of theological development.

Chapter Three focuses on the evolution of Jesus in the pre-modern imagination. I will show the ebb and flow between Jesus as religious icon and emerging iconoclast. Most of these "reincarnations" of Jesus reflect the concerns and sensibilities of the cultures they inhabit. Jesus is remade again and again into the image of his followers. As such we see a reflection of Western history in each new incarnation.

Chapter Four focuses on Jesus as a topic for "Enlightenment" historical consciousness. I will explain how professional historians (both religious and irreligious) have attempted to reconstruct him. In many ways, this era represents a new kind of portraiture. It uses philosophical assumptions and incisive methods to depict Jesus, instead of paint or poetry; but it still reflects the concerns and sensibilities of the artists (even if these historians would rather think of themselves as scientists). A key development at this stage, however, is that historians began to create book-length reconstructions of Jesus's life and aims.

Chapter Five focuses on Jesus in popular (pop) culture. I will show how various contemporary voices utilize Jesus's legacy. These will include ideologues, activists, and artists.

This is a short book on a big topic. While it will map a path from the time of Jesus through to his legacy today, it will trace only one possible route. This guidebook will chart a circuitous way by pointing out just a few landmarks along the trail. Some of these will take us well beyond the beaten path. Hopefully each touchstone will invite more study about the theme, period, or person introduced. As I hope you will see, some variation of Jesus can be found in almost every corner of the Western landscape.

1

Jesus the man

"It seems clear that Jesus understood the anatomy of the relationship between his people and the Romans, and he interpreted that relationship against the background of the profoundest ethical insight of his own religious faith as he had found it in the heart of the prophets of Israel."

Howard Thurman

Introduction: Drop the mike

When scholars talk about Jesus, one phrase always rises to the surface: the "Jesus of history and the Christ of faith." It's a favorite cliché among academics because it allows us to avoid complexity. The basic idea is that Jesus (the man) was some vague or mis-understood philosophy teacher. But Christ (the god-man) is the invention of a new religion. The cliché reduces an interest-ing personality into a boring binary. Worse still, this two-toned umbrella fails to explain how Jesus came to be known as "the Christ." This story requires us to appreciate the immediate and life-changing impact of Jesus. So to illustrate Jesus's impact and evolution, let's look at a modern analogy: Mike King.

In 1929, Michael King was born in Atlanta, Georgia. That year the most famous person from Georgia was baseball legend, Ty

Cobb. The most famous person worldwide was film star, Charlie Chaplin. The biggest news of 1929 was the economic collapse that began with Wall Street investors and exploded into an international catastrophe. Needless to say, very few people took notice when Michael was born. His birth was only good news to the very few people who celebrated.

But within five years Michael's father would rename him, giving him a more symbolic, religious name. In thirty years he would become a famous religious leader. Within forty years he would become an internationally recognized political force. He would be murdered for the controversy he attracted and the politics he represented. Within fifty years he would be a symbolic persona, the ideal for a virtuous and courageous life. Within sixty years he would be one of the most venerated personalities of the modern era. His legacy now easily eclipses Cobb, Chaplin, or any of those Wall Street investors.

"Michael" of course was renamed "Martin Luther": Martin Luther King, Jr. This was the name that would make headlines, create controversy, attract extreme hatred, and extravagant love.

It might be helpful to think of Jesus's historical impact along these lines: born into obscurity; labeled by and conformed to a religious legacy; controversial in public persona; murdered before achieving transcendent status. Most importantly: both Jesus and King had their legacies expanded, transformed, and idealized within decades of their untimely deaths.

MEET THIS WORD: ATONEMENT

Atonement is the state of being reconciled and forgiven from wrongdoing. In theology it refers to a relational reconciliation between God and humankind.

I draw the comparison between King and Jesus because their lives, and what they became posthumously, seem all but impossible. And yet – rare as it might be – sometimes a historical figure embodies the unlikely, the legendary. For example, Jesus is sometimes depicted as a sacrificial lamb (an animal typically offered to God to atone for sin). Here we see Jesus turned into a zoomorphic symbol borrowed from Jewish ritual. Clearly, this sort of depiction is not interested in portraying Jesus, the man. Depicted as a lamb, Jesus represents collective atonement in the Christian imagination. Indeed, many symbols have been used for Jesus: a lamb, a shepherd, a king, a fish, a phoenix, a groom, a loaf of bread, a cup of wine, a gate, a vine, life-giving water, etc.

If Jesus had been born in America in 1929, he would have been depicted with different symbols. Consider the many refractions of Martin Luther King through a modern political prism:

Figure 1 *Lamb of God* (1635): An oil painting on canvas by Spanish artist Francisco de Zurbarán portrays a religious, symbolic subject. In ancient systems of worship, animal sacrifice was often used to appease the gods. In Israelite religion, such sacrifices were supposed to be free from any blemish. In portraying Jesus as a spotless lamb, the Christian imagination associated Jesus's death with sacrifice and his life with perfection. Stylistically it reflects the realism of Amerighi da Caravaggio's school.

heroic underdog, reformer, malcontent, virtuous Christian, white America's favorite symbol of non-violence, Moses, martyr, America's conscience. Some of these symbols distort the man's legacy falsely. And no single symbol captures the man entirely. The story of the transition from Michael to MLK must explain how a kid born in Georgia inspired so many differing opinions about him.

So too with Jesus.

This is why the cliché the "Jesus of history and the Christ of faith" fails. It doesn't hold up any more than a distinction between the "Michael of history" vs. the "MLK of faith" would. Indeed, the life of Jesus helped to shape what his legacy would become. The interested interpreter of history is then left with a puzzle: how do we explain the continuity between Jesus and the multiple portraits of him as Christ? Conversely, how do we account for the fictions that emerged alongside the facts?

It cannot be doubted that both Jesus and King have become idealized symbols. As I write this fifty years later, Martin Luther King is more idea than man. His private doubts and scandals are almost entirely eclipsed by his social impact. His rocky relationships with other African-American religious leaders are all but forgotten. The white America that once thought of him in largely derogatory terms now embraces him (at least a very selective memory of his legacy). In fact, both conservatives and liberals claim him for their side. So too, Jesus had been fictionalized, lionized, idealized, and claimed by multiple ideologies within fifty years of his crucifixion.

Is it possible to sketch a historical portrait while also accounting for these larger-than-life legacies? I believe so. The legacy of King illustrates how a public persona can dramatically evolve in about fifty years. With King, we can measure who he is to us now and critique it. If we are honest and careful we can analyze the legacy fifty years later and judge our own narratives. Scholars of Jesus's life must do something similar with the portraits of

Jesus that we find in Christian commemoration. In many ways, the texts of the New Testament represent Jesus Christ as he had developed twenty to seventy years after his death. Indeed, the gospels that give us the clearest view of Jesus are about fifty years removed from his death.

One key difference between the culture that lionized King and the one that lionized Jesus is that our world includes the invention of secular ideals. People in Jesus's world were more likely to perceive things that we might label supernatural. Important histories were more likely to be wrapped in mythology. *So did people see Jesus perform heavenly signs, or did they create myths about Jesus performing heavenly signs?* The answer is "yes" and "yes." Jesus was a faith healer and a career exorcist. The followers of Jesus, therefore, had every reason to create a mythology around his personality. But the opposite is true of King. Modern-day methods of myth-making are more likely to remove divinity from the story than to add it. Martin Luther King, Jr., grew up the son of a Baptist preacher, was named after a religious founder, went to a seminary, became a preacher himself, was deeply influenced by Gandhi, and collaborated with his friend Rabbi Abraham Heschel. But fifty years after his death, King's religious foundations rarely find expression in contemporary depictions of his life. And the more we remove religious elements from the King story, the less likely we are to find out who he really was.

Both King and Jesus must be understood as men who planted the seeds of a legacy. Most legacies contain clues of the personality from which it derives. The careful and honest student of history must account for the whole picture: both man and myth.

Now we arrive at the nexus of the problem: unless we were compelled by Jesus's legacy, we wouldn't care about him as a man. Or, put another way, if Jesus were just a man like every other man, we wouldn't be interested. The "Christ of faith" will always exist in relationship with the "Jesus of history."

God acts

The first and most important thing to know about Jesus is that he believed in a God of action. Jesus believed in a God who created the heavens and earth. This God would soon judge the wicked and bring justice to the righteous. In this, Jesus was different from most Greek philosophers, Roman intellectual elites, and common folk all over the Mediterranean. This is to say that Jesus – as a Jew of the first century – had a different understanding of God than most of his non-Jewish contemporaries. Jesus was Jewish in his orientation to the Jerusalem Temple and the customs related to this temple. As a Jew, Jesus was forced to negotiate a Greek-speaking world that had a different view of the gods and how they related to the world. The God of Jesus (whom he called "Father") would act on behalf of Israel and all who sought pure worship in the Jerusalem Temple.

Jesus believed in a God of action.

Jesus, as a figure in history, cannot be understood without this simple fact. Like many Jews during this period, Jesus believed that God would soon rule earth in the same way that he ruled the stars. The God who acts would soon act in human political affairs.

MEET THIS WORD: MEDITERRANEAN

Mediterranean refers generally to the Mediterranean Sea or the lands, peoples, and cultures nearby, including North Africa, western Asia, and southern Europe. Jesus lived his entire life in the first-century Mediterranean world during its Roman occupation.

Jesus's followers carried this belief after his death. They called themselves "the Way" and then they called themselves "Christians." But the thread that runs from Jesus to what his following became is the foundational belief that God acts. Jesus's followers (although their beliefs varied) hoped to see God act through Jesus. Some continued to believe this after his execution. They continued to experience God through Jesus even after his death, and preached the good news of his resurrection. In this way, the message of the "gospel" (which literally means "good news") hinged on the belief that during Jesus's death God took action. God, who is first and foremost a Creator, performed a new act of creation in Jesus's body to bring him back to life. Crucially, this divine action served as a sign for things to come.

God's action through Jesus signaled crucial changes in the cosmic order. Political powers would fall and a better government would rise. The disempowered and persecuted would be comforted and made whole. Social hierarchies would reverse. Any person who wanted to worship in God's presence and in perfect purity would be welcomed. Death was not the end.

This was similar to Jesus's public preaching. Jesus preached that his followers must "repent and believe the good news." According to Jesus, "the kingdom of God was at hand." This is a cosmic-political message that God would soon be king – a perfectly righteous king who enacts justice and brings new life. But this good news took a new form once Jesus became a symbol of resurrection. Before his death, Jesus pointed to God as king. After his death, his followers pointed to Jesus as a way into God's kingdom. The central belief that God acts did not change, but this belief was refracted through the prism of Jesus's resurrection.

This is where things get a bit tricky from a historian's perspective. When did the resurrection of Jesus become part of the good news of God's kingdom?

Jesus believed in the coming of God's kingdom – a new world order wherein God would rule on earth as God rules in heaven. He preached about it. He told stories (parables) about it. He prayed about it. But did Jesus imagine that his own resurrection would represent God's primary action?

Figure 2 *Christ Resurrected* (circa 350 CE): In this engraving, Christ is depicted by two Greek letters X (chi) and P (rho) atop a crucifix. These are the first two letters in the Greek word for "Christ." The two Roman soldiers sitting passively below suggest that the resurrected Christ is more powerful than the Roman Empire. Moreover, Christ has conquered Rome's instrument for execution.

The dying and rising of one man seems an unexpected path to a new world order. Jesus might have anticipated his execution, but was resurrection central to his ideology? This question is warranted because Jesus does not talk much about resurrection. It just does not feature prominently (if at all) in his public preaching. Yes, he believed that God would act. But did he know *how* God would act?

Many historians suggest that the early Christians promoted the symbol of resurrection only after Jesus had died (in light of their own experience). Others suggest that Jesus's original preaching was eclipsed by the message of resurrection (thus we don't know much about what Jesus believed). Still others suggest that Jesus understood the significance of his death and resurrection, but did not speak about it in public. If so, the Christians had to reconsider Jesus's teachings in light of God's creative actions. As with any belief system that hinges on divine intervention, past events are seen through the lenses of new experiences.

Jesus and the spirit realm

Jesus's public performances included exorcisms. In fact, he became so famous for them that certain theological titles emerged. And as the stories about Jesus's battle with demons circulated, these theological titles took on apocalyptic scope. Thus, as the rumors spread, Jesus's legend grew.

MEET THIS WORD: COSMOLOGY

A cosmology is a theory of the world/universe that explains how it came into being and the nature of reality. In Jesus's context, most intellectuals assumed a cosmology that included gods (and other divine agents) and featured some kind of creation myth.

Jesus was at war with unclean spirits (also called demons). Many of Jesus's contemporaries believed that spirits could overpower and possess adults, children, buildings, and animals. In this cosmology, unclean spirits could cause illness and erratic behavior.* Jews were not the first people to believe in demonic forces. But in the centuries just before Jesus was born, Jewish storytellers developed mythologies explaining the origins of demons and techniques for their exorcism. While other exorcists used trinkets, tools, special incantations, songs, and other rituals for this purpose, Jesus seemed to be able to cast out unclean spirits by his voice alone. He gained a reputation in Galilee for having an uncanny power over the demonic realm. In one story about Jesus, an onlooker asks, "What is this? A new teaching – with authority! He commands even the unclean spirits, and they obey him." (Mark 1:27).

Such power invites theological speculation. Some of his followers believed that Jesus's authority over these spirits was proof of his spiritual identity. Put another way, some people were convinced that Jesus's authority over cosmic beings revealed his status in the cosmos. When the stories of Jesus's life were told, mundane categories would not do. As Jesus became a storied figure he took on legendary titles.

They called him "Son of David," a title made famous by King Solomon. Solomon was King David's most famous son. Solomon's divinely bestowed wisdom was legendary. But over the course of centuries legends about Solomon had grown. During Jesus's time, King Solomon was the subject of historical fictions. Many of Jesus's contemporaries thought of Solomon as the king of both natural and supernatural wisdom. Solomon – in these myths – knew the right techniques to get rid of demons. Similarly, Jesus seemed to be endowed with heavenly wisdom. So in this way Jesus was like Solomon, and reminiscent of this part of Solomon's legacy.

---

* It is unclear whether Jesus himself believed that demons were the cause of all forms of illness.

Figure 3 Incantation bowl (circa sixth century CE): This ceramic bowl with Aramaic writing is from Nippur, Mesopotamia. The image in the center represents a demon. Such objects were used by exorcists to trap evil spirits. While this bowl postdates Jesus by centuries, Jewish exorcists of the first century used incantations for similar purposes – for instance, psalms for casting out evil spirits have been found among the Dead Sea Scrolls (circa first century).

Then they brought to him a demoniac who was blind and mute; and he cured him, so that the one who had been mute could speak and see. All the crowds were amazed and said, "Can this be the Son of David?" (Matt. 12:22–3)

Other popular Jewish stories explained political events with mythic categories like great beasts, dragons, and demonic forces. Jesus's reputation as a person with cosmic power probably inspired the title "Son of Man" – the cosmic being mentioned by the prophet Daniel. According to Daniel's vision a figure like a "Son of Man" had divine authority to subdue Israel's enemies. As these stories circulated, Jesus was called "Son of God." This was the title with the most traction. It was a mythological category, but it framed a historical figure. In so doing, this marriage of myth and history would cement Jesus within the foundations of Western civilization.

Before Jesus, this mythological title was claimed by Caesar Augustus (who claimed to be the adopted son of the deified Julius). But to gain a fuller understanding of this title and to understand better how Jesus emerged as a cosmic figure, we need to hear a story that was popular during Jesus's time. Here is a summary:

> Long ago, when the world was young, heavenly beings called the "sons of God" had sex with human women. The offspring of this hybrid union were monstrous. Sometimes they were called giants; sometimes they were called the Fallen Ones. They taught humankind to do evil and they spread chaos and violence. This was during the time of Noah, and God could not abide the spread of evil among and by humans. God opened the floodgates of heaven and a great flood wiped almost all living creatures from the land. Noah, his family, and many animals were saved to repopulate the earth. The evil giants sunk under the waters and died, but the souls of the giants survived in disembodied form. A number of these spirits still roam the earth today as unclean demons.*

---

* This mythology is an expansion of Genesis 6:1–4. Extended narratives can be read in 1 Enoch and Jubilees.

Chances are that Jesus heard this story told around the campfire or in the public square. It is a story that functions much like the story of Pandora's Box. It explained so many of the problems in the world, including illness, corruption, and impurity. It explained how Satan – the spiritual enemy of God and Israel – wielded so much power. Jesus believed that in order for God's new world order to be a pure kingdom the unclean spirits would need to be cast out.

This mixing of politics and the spirit realm will seem odd from a modern, Western perspective. But we must remember how important storytelling is for worldview construction. In my life, I have heard, read, and watched hundreds of underdog stories. These are stories of people of low social rank rising up and grasping a boon far beyond expectation. Love stories are equally ubiquitous. How many stories do we tell about people falling in and out of love? These stories are not benign entertainment; they are narratives by which we measure our own lives, assess our worth, and judge the virtues of others. Jesus's culture constructed a different sort of worldview by internalizing stories about fallen angels, Solomon's wisdom, and the return of God as judge.

Jesus as healer

It was common in Jesus's time to think that illness was the result of demonic interference. This does not mean that demons were always associated with illness, but there was enough overlap for Jesus to gain a reputation as a healer. Jesus was reputed to heal hemorrhaging and all sorts of physical deformities, to give sight to the blind, and even raise the dead. Thus his reputation as a healer crossed the border into legendary stories. Among his contemporaries, this sort of reputation would have been associated with divine activity.

MEET THIS WORD: SCRIBE

In Jesus's culture, scribes were language and scripture experts. Over 95 percent of people were illiterate. While common people might be able to read a shopping list or write their names, sacred texts or literary epics were beyond the expertise of most. So scribes were arbiters of knowledge. Being an elite scribe (as employed by a king, a high priest, or a philosopher) meant occupying a position of great influence.

Consider this passage from a Jewish scribe named Ben Sira, written a few generations before Jesus:

> Honor physicians for their services, for the Lord created them; for their gift of healing comes from the Most High, and they are rewarded by the king. The skill of physicians makes them distinguished, and in the presence of the great they are admired. The Lord created medicines out of the earth, and the sensible will not despise them... And he gave skill to human beings that he might be glorified in his marvelous works. By them the physician heals and takes away pain; the pharmacist makes a mixture from them. God's works will never be finished; and from him health spreads over all the earth. (Sirach 38:1–8)

In this description, the gift of healing is associated with God's power. At the same time, the healer's work is described in very naturalistic ways: "medicines out of the earth." These two points may seem contradictory to the modern mind. But this is not the way that Ben Sira thinks. The making of medicine is not necessarily distinct from God's involvement. Ben Sira continues: "There may come a time when recovery lies in the hands of physicians, for they too pray to the Lord that he grant them success in diagnosis and in healing, for the sake of preserving life" (38:13–14). Healers in the ancient world did not usually see their activities as a distinct field apart from God's actions. Even so, it is likely that Ben Sira has little more than folk medicine in mind.

Again, Jesus's reputation takes on legendary status. One noteworthy difference is that Jesus does not use roots, herbs, or devices (like incantation bowls or trinkets). Jesus's method – as it is described in later narratives of his life – was to employ the power of his voice. It was as if he commanded healing by the spoken word. In some cases the Gospel of Mark records Jesus's healing words in Aramaic. Once Jesus says *talitha koum*, which means "get up, little girl" (Mark 5:41). Jesus also says *ephphatha*, which means "be opened" (Mark 7:34). It is also noteworthy that for the Greek-speaking readers of Mark, these words might have seemed mystical and spiritual simply because they were exotic. In some cases, however, Jesus would touch the person, or use his own spit or mix it into the dirt to make mud. Perhaps then, we see something closer to what Ben Sira describes as "medicines out of the earth."

What did Jesus look like?

Medieval and modern depictions of Jesus show him in many variations. But the usual theme is so recognizable it has become iconic: long hair, tanned or pale skin, bearded, robed with heavy, flowing sleeves. But what did the Jesus of history look like?

The fact that we have no commentary on Jesus's physical description from anyone who knew him suggests that Jesus's physicality was unremarkable. So by way of a sociologically informed guess, we are on safe ground to suggest that Jesus looked very similar to his contemporaries. This would rule out the iconic "Jesus look" made popular by artists throughout the centuries.

Jesus probably had short, curly hair. His skin would have been darker than most European-influenced depictions of him. Jesus probably went sleeveless and his tunic wouldn't have extended beyond his knees.* Consider this statement that Jesus makes about his contemporary, John the Baptist:

> When John's messengers had gone, Jesus began to speak to the crowds about John: "What did you go out into the wilderness to look at? A reed shaken by the wind? What then did you go out to see? Someone dressed in soft robes? Look, those who put on fine clothing and live in luxury are in royal palaces." (Luke 7:24–5)

It is possible that Jesus dressed like those who "live in luxury," but – given what we know of his lifestyle and social class – this is highly unlikely. Jesus's statement about John's attire therefore tells us something about his own attire: the iconic bleach-white robes with flowing sleeves are probably a fiction.

Also consider this fact: the average height of a male in Jesus's world was about 5 feet 6 inches. It is possible that Jesus was exceptionally tall, but we have no evidence of this. Think of it this way: Jesus could have been five foot four and nobody would have considered it unusual.

It is impossible to know whether Jesus wore a beard or not. While European artists generally depicted him with a full beard (see my treatment of **The Letter of Lentulus** later), in later periods archeologists have discovered depictions of a beardless Jesus. These can be dated as early as the fourth century. This style seems to be in keeping with that of the first century. Indeed, the use of razors for facial upkeep is a very old practice and one that went in and out of fashion in the ancient world.

Meticulous care of one's teeth is a modern invention. Oral hygiene in Jesus's day may have included some form of twig for scraping and chewing. It would have been quite common for regular folk to have missing teeth. Whereas many modern minds

---

* For more on this topic, see Taylor, J.E., *What Did Jesus Look Like?* (London: T&T Clark, 2017).

Figure 4 Fourth-century mural of Jesus: Found in the Catacombs of Marcellinus and Peter in Rome, it depicts Jesus healing a hemorrhaging woman (Luke 8). Many early depictions of Jesus picture him without a beard, as he is shown here.

associate a straight, white, full set of teeth a requirement for social normalcy, this was not the case in Jesus's world.

So what would a socio-historical best guess be for Jesus's appearance? If Jesus walked into a modern coffee shop, he would look – to our eyes – like this: small, dark skin, sleeveless, short tunic, no beard, teeth missing. And, of course, if he carried enough shekels to afford a latte, he would order it in Aramaic or Hebrew.

Jesus was Jewish

It is often assumed that Jesus was the first Christian. After all, the name "Christ" became Jesus's honorific title among his follow-ers, and from this title we get the word "Christian." But Jesus, the man, never heard the word "Christian." He most certainly wouldn't have described himself as such. Jesus's identity was defined first and foremost with the culture of Jerusalem as it extended in influence to the Jews of Galilee. Not only was Jesus Jewish, he was always Jewish, and remained Jewish in the minds of his earliest devotees (who were also Jewish).

MEET THIS WORD: CHRISTIAN

The title Christian, according to the New Testament, was first employed by a group in Antioch of Syria. "The disciples were called Christians first in Antioch" (Acts 11:26). The root of the word is the Hebrew word mashah, which is the term for ritual anointing. A messiah [mashiah], in Jewish thought, was an anointed leader (kings, priests, and prophets could be anointed). Many of Jesus's early followers believed him to be a messiah. The title Mashiah translated into Greek is Christos, from which the title Christ derives. Thus a Christian is one who is devoted to Christ (designating Jesus's messianic status).

Jesus's Jewishness is important for understanding how Jesus thought of God and his own mission. It is also important that we do not project our modern notions of nationality, ethnicity, and religion onto Jesus. To be Jewish in Jesus's time and place meant to be oriented to the customs, worship, and legal practices of Jerusalem. Jesus would have understood his life, significance, and mission within the orbit of the Jerusalem Temple. In this world-view, the Jerusalem Temple was unlike any other temple on earth. It was where heaven and earth met. It was the only place on earth where God's glorified presence could dwell. Jesus believed that God's kingdom would be established on the earth, and that Jerusalem would be the capital.

Figure 5 The Magdala Stone (circa first century CE): This decorative stone was displayed in a synagogue (a gathering place) in Migdal, near the Sea of Galilee. A seven-lamped menorah is showcased symbolizing the Jerusalem Temple (over sixty miles south). This symbol hints that the Jews who gathered here were mindful of, and oriented to, Temple worship.

There were a variety of ways that a Jew could orient toward the Jerusalem Temple. Some Jews lived and worked within the holy city. Some Jews lived in foreign cities – for instance, among other Jews in northern Africa – their entire lives, but continued to look toward Jerusalem for collective meaning and practice. Some Jews made a pilgrimage to Jerusalem to worship at the Temple for festivals. As a Galilean Jew, Jesus was close enough to the city to travel to it on occasion. Still, he would have been different in a number of ways from the power brokers and urbanites of the Jerusalem Temple establishment. Toward the end of his life, Jesus picked a fight with those wealthy power brokers. But this conflict was not an assault on Judaism; both Jesus and his adversaries were deeply invested in the well-being of the holy city and the people within its orbit.

Jews – while they shared in common their connection to the Holy City – varied in their city orientations.* Some Jews were upset with Jerusalem's leadership because Rome – a foreign, imperial force – had too much influence. Some Jews moved to the desert and longed for a day when the Temple could be purified from foreign influence. Some Jews looked to heaven,

---

* I am going to avoid simplistic definitions of the various "schools of thought," e.g. Pharisees, Sadducees, Essenes. While attempts to define these sects by ideological difference are commonplace in introductions to the Second Temple period (this era begins in the late sixth century BCE and concludes with the destruction of the Temple in 70 CE.), I find these to be misleading. Variance in city and/or Temple orientation is a more accurate way to think of the differences in these groups. In Jesus's day, the Sadducees were influential leaders of Jerusalem. Pharisees tended to be regional teachers and friends with the common folk. Essenes (at least some) were critics of the Temple establishment. Some within the Qumran sect believed themselves to be the true priesthood. These should not be thought of as religious denominations. They are, rather, differences of Temple orientation.

where a mirror image (in purer form) of the Jerusalem Temple was attended by angels. Still other Jews were happy with the *status quo* of Rome's influence. I would imagine many Jews – occupied with farming and feeding their families – did not involve themselves in matters of statecraft or voice opinions on the topic. It is a matter of debate among scholars *which* of these types best describes Jesus. But the fact remains that Jesus was indeed oriented toward Jerusalem and was therefore Jewish. He was so not only by birth, but also by way of politics, worship, and custom.

Jesus and the Pharisees

In the earliest gospels, Jesus is portrayed in repeated conversation with the Pharisees. While not every dialogue is a debate, most of these exchanges are argumentative. At times they are quite heated. This has led to a common misunderstanding about Pharisees. If you look up "Pharisee" on Dictionary.com, you will find two definitions:

1. a member of a Jewish sect that flourished during the 1st century b.c. and 1st century a.d. and that differed from the Sadducees chiefly in its strict observance of religious ceremonies and practices, adherence to oral laws and traditions, and belief in an afterlife and the coming of a messiah.
2. *(lowercase)* a sanctimonious, self-righteous, or hypocritical person.*

The first definition is almost right. If measured by political influence and status, the Pharisees flourished most during the reign of Salome Alexandra (Queen of Judea, circa 70 BCE). After Salome passed her reign to her sons, the Pharisees were replaced by the

---

* http://www.dictionary.com/browse/pharisee

Sadducees as the power brokers of Jerusalem. The Sadducees were experts on the interpretation of Jewish law and its application to Jewish life. The key difference between the Sadducees and Pharisees was not necessarily ideological, but political. The Sadducees enjoyed a great deal of political influence in Jerusalem in Jesus's day. The Pharisees, on the other hand, were more allied with the common folk. There are examples of both Sadducees and Pharisees who strictly observed Jewish laws and traditions, but there is no reason to think that strict observance was unique to one group or the other. We should also assume that there were some Pharisees and some Sadducees who were less strict.

MEET THIS WORD: RABBI

During Jesus's time, rabbi was not an official title but was used as a term of respect for distinguished and educated experts. The word derives from the Hebrew word *rav*, meaning "great" or "distinguished one." When the suffix *i* is added, *rabbi* literally means "*my* distinguished one." In Mark 10:51, a blind man calls Jesus *rabbouni*, which means "my distinguished one" in Aramaic. In later periods, rabbi was used as a title for professionally educated legal teachers and appointed community leaders.

This brings us to the second (lower case) definition. The modern, Christianized West has repeated an anti-Jewish definition of the Pharisees so often, the term has become a slur. It is generally true that the Pharisees were law-observant. So too was Jesus. Matthew, in particular, casts Jesus in this light: "whoever breaks one of the least of these commandments, and teaches others to do the same, will be called least in the kingdom of heaven; but whoever does them and teaches them will be called great in the kingdom of heaven" (Matt. 5:19).

It is also possible that — at times — both Jesus and the Pharisees attempted to summarize and simplify Jewish laws for the sake of their audiences. Consider one of Jesus's more well-known sayings: "In everything do to others as you would have them do to you; for this is the law and the prophets" (Matt. 7:12). This is often called the "golden rule."

Was Jesus innovative in simplifying Jewish scripture into a single life ethic? A story from a sacred Jewish text that postdates the time of Jesus might provide some clues. While it might postdate Jesus by hundreds of years, the Babylonian Talmud reaches back into history to recall two schools of Pharisees just before Jesus was born. Some Pharisees followed a rabbi named Shammai, and others followed a rabbi named Hillel.

> It happened that a certain heathen came before Shammai and said to him, "Make me a proselyte [i.e. a convert], on condition that you teach me the whole Torah while I stand on one foot." Thereupon he [Shammai] repulsed him with the builder's cubit [a rod] which was in his hand. When he went before Hillel, he said to him, "What is hateful to you, do not to your neighbor: that is the whole Torah, while the rest is the commentary thereof; go and learn it." (Tractate Shabat 31a)

This story tells of two competing rabbis: Hillel and Shammai. Much of the legacy of Hillel and Shammai reflects the concerns of rabbinic Judaism of a later period (favoring Hillel). But this story may also tell us something about the complexity of first-century Pharisaic thought at the time of Jesus. If so, some rabbis were quite happy to sum the instructions of Moses (for non-Jews) into a simple "golden rule," while others wanted to preserve their complexity (making adherence to Jewish law more difficult for outsiders). Hillel is able to reduce and simplify as a first step toward understanding Jewish life. Shammai took offense at the suggestion that such a lesson was possible as a student stood "on one foot." Presumably a lesson taught while the student balances on one foot is a short lesson. The question becomes, then, *Can a non-Jew learn what is important about Jewish life in one short, simple lesson?* Judging from this story, Hillel was willing to try; Shammai was not (we might also keep in mind that Shammai's "builder's cubit" might be a metaphor for the law itself).

I have pointed to a similar golden rule attributed to Jesus: "So whatever you wish that others would do to you, do also to them." These golden rules aren't exactly the same, but they are similar. And, to the point: both Jesus and Hillel are willing to attempt a summary statement. We could say that, in this case, Jesus seems to have more in common with Hillel than he does with Shammai. This comparison illustrates that Jesus sounds like at least one Pharisee of the first century, and that there was also a variety of ways to be a Pharisee in the first century. We should not assume that just because Jesus argues with certain Pharisees in the gospels that he was altogether different from them.

Jesus and food

One of the most widespread commemorations of Jesus's teaching among early Christians is his institution of a ritual meal. Modern Christians often call this the "Last Supper" or "Holy Communion." As early Christians ate and drank bread and wine, they remembered Jesus's broken and bleeding body. (See more in the section titled **The meal of Jesus** later.) It is then possible to see food as a metaphor for spiritual nourishment. Jesus's followers believed that consuming the sacred bread and wine placed them in the very presence of God.

Jesus also assumes that those who follow his teaching will share food with each other (Luke 11:5–12). "Is there anyone among you who, if your child asks for a fish, will give a snake instead of a fish? Or if the child asks for an egg, will give a scorpion?" Jesus assumes that even the most imperfect members of his group will provide for their children. He likens this to his "Father" in heaven who provides something like spiritual nourishment. But Jesus does not always spiritualize food. Sometimes he is simply concerned with the physical nourishment of those who lack daily food. Consider this teaching:

> When the Son of Man comes in his glory, and all the angels with him, then he will sit on the throne of his glory... Then the king will say to those at his right hand, "Come, you that are blessed by my Father, inherit the kingdom prepared for you from the foundation of the world; for I was hungry and you gave me food, I was thirsty and you gave me something to drink, I was a stranger and you welcomed me, I was naked and you gave me clothing, I was sick and you took care of me, I was in prison and you visited me." Then the righteous will answer him, "Lord, when was it that we saw you hungry and gave you food, or thirsty and gave you something to drink? And when was it that we saw you a stranger and welcomed you, or naked and gave you clothing? And when was it that we saw you sick or in prison and visited you?" And the king will answer them, "Truly I tell you, just as you did it to one of the least of these who are members of my family, you did it to me." Then he will say to those at his left hand, "You that are accursed, depart from me into the eternal fire prepared for the devil and his angels; for I was hungry and you gave me no food, I was thirsty and you gave me nothing to drink, I was a stranger and you did not welcome me, naked and you did not give me clothing, sick and in prison and you did not visit me." Then they also will answer, "Lord, when was it that we saw you hungry or thirsty or a stranger or naked or sick or in prison, and did not take care of you?" Then he will answer them, "Truly I tell you, just as you did not do it to one of the least of these, you did not do it to me." And these will go away into eternal punishment, but the righteous into eternal life. (Matt. 25:31–46)

This teaching assumes a Divine Judge expectation that was common in Jewish thought. In this case, Jesus suggests that doing right by the stranger, the naked, the sick, the prisoner, the thirsty and hungry, is a requirement for eternal life. As such, the sharing of physical food is a necessity for both the giver and the receiver.

MEET THIS WORD: ESCHATOLOGY

Eschatology is a hope, theory, or doctrine about final things. The word derives from the Greek word *eschatos*, meaning "last" or "extreme." Within a theological system, eschatology refers to beliefs about the last days. More specifically, it is the study of the end of time and space as we know it. Many historical Jesus scholars think that Jesus was preoccupied with the end of the world and, therefore, was motivated by a strong eschatological belief. Jesus's followers hoped for his "second coming," the belief that Jesus would return before the end of days.

There is another reason why food was significant for Jesus and his disciples. The idea of a great feast was an important symbol in Jewish eschatology. Many contemporaries of Jesus believed that after the final judgment, the righteous would celebrate with a feast. This was conceived as an end-of-days party. Jesus, who frequented parties often, might have enacted this symbolism. It could be that Jesus and his disciples celebrated with food and wine as a foretaste of things to come.

Finally, another important element of food in Jesus's teaching relates to practices of "purity" within day-to-day Jewish life. On this, see the section below.

Jesus and purity

Many (perhaps all) of Jesus's contemporaries who lived in and practiced day-to-day Jewish life believed that their God was transcendent. Not only was God separate from and above the created order, God was holy and pure in a way that fundamentally distinguished God from the world of humans. In the priestly story of creation, the elements of the earth are said to be good. But only God is holy. Thus we see a very ancient worldview distinction between that which is *common* and that which is *holy*. In Jewish tradition, in order to prepare for the worship of a holy God, rites of purity were practiced.

Unfortunately, the common elements of creation are subject to disorder and eventual death. Humanity – while fundamentally good – is prone to disorder and dominated by death. Many Jewish texts before and during Jesus's period address the problems of impurity. These problems are, according to Jewish tradition, the consequences of living in a world subjected to disorder and death. Impurity, because it is linked with death, is a power opposed to life; it is an infection that results in physical, ritual, and moral disease.* God, on the other hand, is holy and pure.

The Exodus tradition – the story that provided the foundation of Israel's collective identity – claims that God is holy, and it is dangerous for humans to be in God's presence. Indeed, only Moses is initially allowed to see God and, even then, Moses cannot look at God face-to-face. God, however, provided a way for the Israelites to participate in God's life-giving holiness. During

---

* It is important to make a distinction between impurity and sin. Ritual impurity was inevitable, and in most cases had nothing to do with human error. Childbirth, disease, contact with the dead, and bodily fluid caused impurity. Such elements of human life and death were not necessarily sinful, but required purification through rituals. Moreover, these rituals (like baptism) were not difficult to accomplish. Moral impurity, on the other hand, was connected with human error: e.g. worship of idols (Lev. 19:31; 20:1–3); sexual taboo (Lev. 18:24–30); murder (Num. 35:33–4). In very basic terms, most of the rituals practiced in Jewish life related to the maintenance of life and death – or, at least, the elements that seemed most related to life and death (e.g. blood, semen, menstruation, food production). Much of the first part of Leviticus deals with ritual purification as it relates to Temple worship (the place where God resides on earth). Much of the second half of Leviticus deals with broader issues of purity in everyday life (what scholars call the Holiness Code).

the Exodus from Egypt, God gave the Israelites instructions for purifying rituals. This is first accomplished by Moses, who follows divine instructions for creating a space for the transcendent God to reside on earth. The "Tabernacle" – a mobile tent-like structure – functioned as the Temple for this nomadic people. It was then imperative for the priests to prepare the common people to approach this holy space. Thus, certain rituals were established to cleanse the people from impurity. Purity is therefore integral to the human–divine encounter.

The holy site was built up as a Temple. In this culture, God was thought to be present in the Jerusalem Temple. Instructions for pure living helped to orient the people to God's Temple presence. Everyday actions like food, sex, farming, care for strangers, etc., became ways to orient the people to the holy presence of God.

In Jesus's time, almost every Jew – whether living in Jerusalem, Idumea, Africa, or beyond – was oriented to the Jerusalem Temple in some way. Some sent money for the purchase and sacrifice of an animal. Some (like many in Galilee) would travel to Jerusalem to celebrate festivals and worship in the Temple. Some Jews preserved images (engraved in stone) of the Temple's lampstands in their local synagogues to remind them of God's presence in Jerusalem. Some Jews (like the elite Sadducees) held sway over Temple politics. Others (like those at Qumran) stood in opposition to the Jerusalem Temple establishment.

Jesus, by every indication, had a keen interest in the Jerusalem Temple. He seems to have traveled to Jerusalem to worship on occasion. He had strong opinions about how the Temple funds were being used. Most scholars argue that while Jesus had great reverence for the institution of the Temple, he expressed criticism of the elite members of the Temple establishment. If so, Jesus would have been keenly interested in the purity rituals practiced by those in the Temple's orbit.

The ritual baptisms of "John the Baptist" are an example of purity practice. The fact of Jesus's baptism by John indicates Jesus's concern for purity. Jesus seems to have argued about how to conduct various purity rituals with some of the Pharisees. For example:

> One sabbath he [Jesus] was going through the cornfields; and as they made their way his disciples began to pluck heads of grain. The Pharisees said to him, "Look, why are they doing what is not lawful on the sabbath?" And he said to them, "Have you never read what David did when he and his companions were hungry and in need of food? He entered the house of God, when Abiathar was high priest, and ate the bread of the Presence, which it is not lawful for any but the priests to eat, and he gave some to his companions." (Mark 2:23–6)

Jesus's logic might seem odd but remember that rituals like observing a holy day of rest and eating with ritual purity were ways to orient to the Temple. Jesus points to David, who was not only oriented to the Temple but *inside* the Temple. Moreover, not only did David eat improperly, he ate food dedicated to God in the very presence of God. By using this example, Jesus was appealing to a loophole in legal instruction. In this case, Jesus argued that his disciples were not guilty of breaking purity laws. This too suggests that Jesus was invested in the topic of purity. Jesus, in some cases, may well have had a relatively unorthodox view of these rituals, but he remained deeply concerned with matters of ritual purity.

Jesus and the Roman Empire

Jewish life in the first-century was lived in the shadow of the Roman Empire. In Judea, Galilee, and all over the Mediterranean, Jews lived under the rule of Rome. There were, however, varying and divergent Jewish attitudes toward the Empire. Many Jews continued with their agrarian lives without voicing any protest. Some retreated to the wilderness. Some benefited from Roman dominance and affluence through alliance. Some attempted to fully assimilate into Roman culture. Some established resistance movements.

Jesus probably encountered Rome in various ways. He most likely witnessed the rise of Roman architecture on the Galilean landscape. He certainly would have known that the Lake of Kinneret (also called the Sea of Galilee) had been renamed for the Roman Caesar, Tiberias. The coins Jesus used at the market had the image of the Caesar on them. Jesus probably encountered Roman soldiers on the roads and in the marketplace. Shortly before Jesus was born, a group of Galileans – thought to be troublemakers – had been violently subdued and summarily executed. Jesus might have heard the stories of their bravery, or laments about their fate. Even if Jesus never entered a place of Roman worship, or spoke with a Roman intellectual, he would have seen the presence of Rome all around him.

MEET THIS WORD: GOSPEL

Gospel is a word with multiple facets. It literally means "good news." For example, "Jesus came to Galilee, proclaiming the good news of God" (Mark 1:14). Or, "The Lord has sent me to preach good news to the oppressed" (Isa. 61:1). It comes from the Greek word *euangelion*, and can refer to any kind of favorable message. But the term also carried a Roman, imperial connotation. Caesar Augustus (63 BCE–14 CE) made the term popular in political propaganda. In this sense, a "gospel" was a report of a military advancement by the Roman Empire. It is possible that Jesus subverts this idea when he announces that God's kingdom is advancing. Because of Jesus's use of the term, the first biographies of Jesus (Matthew, Mark, Luke, and John) were called "gospels." From the second to the sixth centuries CE, many other short documents were written (not necessarily biographies) about Jesus. These are now called "Apocryphal gospels."

Jesus's most direct encounter with Rome happened in Jerusalem. As Israel's center of social, fiscal, and sacred power, the Empire was interested in the politics of Jerusalem. As such, Herod (Idumean by birth) had been propped up as *de facto* middle management between Rome and the people of Judea. From a political point of view, Herod was a great success. To fortify his power and legacy, he expanded and improved the Jerusalem Temple. The grandeur of the architecture was reputed all over the Empire. But many Jews viewed Herod as a puppet for foreign occupation, and thus a corrupting influence. For Jews, the Temple was meant to be the holiest (and thus purest) place on earth. But many questioned Roman interference: *If the Sadducees, priests, and Herodians were puppets for the Empire, how "pure" is the Jerusalem Temple?* Regardless of how one answered this question, one thing was clear: the most obvious point of intersection between the Roman Empire and Jewish life was in the Jerusalem Temple.

When Jesus approached Jerusalem, Rome's influence would have been unmistakable. First, the holiest place on earth was also a monument to Herod's legacy. Second, right next to the Temple precincts was the Fortress of Antonia, a Roman military tower built on the eastern wall and constructed to be just taller than the Holy of Holies. Third, the architecture proclaimed extravagant wealth. This may well have reminded Jesus that Rome continually drew funds from the Temple treasury.

Jesus is remembered for predicting the Temple's destruction (Mark 13:1–2; John 2:19). He was also seen turning over tables used for coin exchange. The reason for Jesus's public demonstration on the Temple's grounds is a matter of debate among scholars. But we will be on the right track when we consider the impurity caused by Rome's greed at the very place where God is meant to be worshipped. The Gospel of Mark also interprets Jesus's protest like this:

> Then they came to Jerusalem. And he entered the temple and began to drive out those who were selling and those who were buying in the temple, and he overturned the tables of the money changers and the seats of those who sold doves; and he would not allow anyone to carry anything through the temple. He was teaching and saying, "Is it not written, 'My house shall be called a house of prayer for all the nations?' But you have made it a den of robbers." (Mark 11:15–17)

This action had dire consequences for Jesus. As a result, Jesus was arrested and eventually placed under Roman authority. Shortly after, Mark portrays Jesus in dialogue with Pontius Pilate (Rome's governing representative in Judea). While Mark seems to exonerate Pilate's guilt (Mark 15:14–15), the fact remains: Jesus ended up on a Roman cross, executed by Roman hands.

Jesus prays

In the earliest stories of Jesus's life, he is depicted as a person who prayed directly to God as a son would speak to his father. The narrators of Jesus's life often show Jesus praying before episodes of divine action. For example, Jesus prays before hearing a voice from heaven, before healing ill people, and before walking on water. He also prays before and during major events in the narrative, such as his baptism, his "last supper" (a ritual meal with his disciples before his death), and from the cross.

Jesus is also depicted as a person who often prays in private. The Gospel of Luke reports that Jesus retreated from the crowds to be alone: "he would withdraw to deserted places and pray" (5:16). Rather than going to a specific place of worship or a public setting, Jesus seems to have preferred the wilderness and solitude. This may, in part, explain why his disciples must ask Jesus to teach them how to pray. They have not been present to observe many of his prayers, and Jesus, perhaps, prayed in ways that were uncommon. "He was praying in a certain place, and after he had finished, one of his disciples said to him, 'Lord, teach us to pray, as John taught his disciples' " (Luke 11:1). Seemingly, John the Baptist had instructed his followers on prayer, but Jesus had not.

In the Gospel of Matthew, Jesus instructs his disciples not to pray in public. He claims that "hypocrites" pray "so that they may be seen by others" (Matt. 6:5). This saying contributes to the portrait of Jesus as a person of private prayer. It is also possible that the narrative intends to distance Jesus from other Jewish leaders, as this is a key theme in Matthew. While we should not imagine too much difference between Jesus and other Jewish leaders, Jesus's method of prayer may well have required explanation, simply because it appeared different.

One of Jesus's private prayers is depicted in Mark 14:

> They went to a place called Gethsemane; and he said to his disciples, "Sit here while I pray." He took with him Peter and James and John, and began to be distressed and agitated. And he said to them, "I am deeply grieved, even to death; remain here, and keep awake." And going a little farther, he threw himself on the ground and prayed that, if it were possible, the hour might pass from him. He said, "Abba, Father, for you all things are possible; remove this cup from me; yet, not what I want, but what you want."

At this place in the story, Jesus is aware of his impending death and wants to, again, pray alone. This is a story about how the disciples fail to stay awake to pray or keep watch. But this passage also reveals a few details of Jesus's private prayer. He calls God "abba," which means "father." Jesus refers to his impending execution as "this cup," and asks for an alternative. Jesus believes that it is possible for his "Father" to save him from his public shaming and execution. This prayer also suggests that Jesus's request is unmet; God does not save him. The story reports that Jesus repeated the prayer three times. Directly after, Jesus is arrested.

When Jesus prays from the cross, he shouts, "My God, my God, why have you forsaken me?" (Mark 15:34).

After reading the gospels, one may be left with the impression that Jesus has an especially intimate relationship with his heavenly Father. The voice from heaven says, "You are my Son, the Beloved; with you I am well pleased" (Mark 1:11). Jesus's life of prayer probably reinforces this intimacy. If indeed these narratives are meant to convey this theme, it reaches a negative climax at the crucifixion. Unexpectedly, Jesus's prayers are not answered.

Why did the Romans kill Jesus?

One popular notion of Jesus in modern times is that he was a teacher and preacher of love. This may be partially true. Jesus was a preacher, and he did reinforce Jewish tradition by saying, "You shall love the Lord your God with all your heart, and with all your soul, and with all your mind. This is the greatest and first commandment. And a second is like it: you shall love your neighbor as yourself" (Matt. 22:34–9). So it is true that Jesus taught on the topic of love. But this is not the whole of his message. Preaching about love alone does not explain why Jesus was executed.

Rome did not execute people for talking about love. While it is true that Jesus did sometimes talk about love, the gospels also show him to be argumentative. Moreover, he often argued with those of higher social standing. Even so, Jesus does not often argue with Romans. So why did the Romans crucify him?

Scholars of previous generations said that crucifixion was the slave's death or, contrarily, that it was reserved for insurrectionists. But these short explanations do not quite hit the mark. It would be more accurate to say that crucifixion (i.e. nailed to a post or cross and hung in public) was a way to shame people who had "risen above" their station. There was, therefore, a presumption

MEET THIS WORD: IRONY

Irony is an expression that conveys meaning by saying the opposite from what is expected. In verbal form, an ironic expression conveys the opposite of the literal meaning of the words used. Dramatic irony often involves speech used in a story that the audience understands, but the characters within the story fail to grasp. An example of dramatic irony might be found in John 12:32. Jesus says, "when I am lifted up from the earth, will draw all people to myself." The literal words speak of exaltation, but the narrator explains that Jesus was speaking about how he will die.

of class hierarchy. If a person of lower social standing had exalted himself, crucifixion was a grotesque parody of this self-exalting.

Slaves who murdered their masters might be crucified. Common folk who demonstrated disrespect for Caesar might be crucified. So, of course, open revolt against imperial rule might result in a crucifixion, or several. If indeed the leader of an insurrection found himself on a cross, it would be an ironically high station. It was almost as if the Roman authorities were saying with sarcasm: "You think that you'd make a good king? Let us help you elevate yourself." In short, it was a way to mock those of lower standing who aspired to be greater.

With this in mind, consider the sign nailed above Jesus's cross: "KING OF THE JEWS." This sign, meant to mock Jesus, tells us at least two important things about him. First, Jesus was viewed by some to have royal aspirations. Second, Jesus's crucifixion was an ironic demonstration of his failure as he was both "exalted" and "put down" at the same time. At least some Roman authorities believed that Jesus had risen above his social rank and thus warranted crucifixion.

It is highly likely that Jesus was mocked as "KING OF THE JEWS" because he was known for preaching about the coming of God's kingdom. Even if misunderstood, Jesus did in fact "get above" himself with this politically charged message. If the divinely endorsed king of Israel was just around the corner – and this is how Jesus would have been heard – this might be perceived as a threat to Roman ears.

Was Jesus a messiah?

The word "messiah" derives from the idea of anointing. It is important to recognize the Hebrew tradition that gives meaning to this concept. A good place to start is with King David. The story of David's anointing (a ritual sometimes used like a royal coronation) is found in 1 Samuel of the Hebrew Bible. 1 Sam. 16:13 reads: "Then Samuel took the horn of oil and anointed him in the midst of his brothers; and the spirit of the Lord came mightily upon David from that day forward."

David's legacy was marked by the actions of God through him, with him, and (sometimes) against him. Eventually the Israelites came to believe that David's kingship would last forever. This belief evolved into the idea of a future "messiah" who was expected to restore Israel's kingdom and worship to an ideal state. The word messiah literally means "anointed one," and is translated to Greek as *christos*. Thus we see the roots of Jesus's title "Christ."

There is a common notion (made popular by previous generations of scholarship) that first-century Jews expected the Messiah to be a conqueror like David. But this notion is simplistic, overstated, or simply false. Some Jews may have expected a military figure to rise up. It is unclear, however, what sort of war was anticipated. Was it to be a literal war against Rome? Was it to be a heavenly war fought by spirits? Or maybe a combination of both? Would the God of Israel – as divine warrior – defeat Israel's enemies? Or would the Messiah do this as an agent of God? Moreover, it is unclear how widespread this sort of militant messianism was. Other Jews of the first century (for example, those who collected and authored the Dead Sea Scrolls) anticipated multiple messiahs. One among them would be a priestly messiah. It is also possible that some expected an anointed prophet. If so, there was a hope for three messiah figures: one royal, one priestly, and one prophetic.

So how does Jesus fit into this ideology? Jesus does talk often about the "kingdom (or rule) of God." He also refers to himself as "son of man." Son of man might have referred to the heavenly figure in the Hebrew prophetic tradition (Daniel 7) who would – echoing King David – receive an "everlasting kingdom." It is possible, therefore, that Jesus thought of himself in messianic terms. Whatever the case, Jesus's disciples had to rethink the category of messiah after Jesus was crucified because there was no expectation of this. The notion of "Christ crucified" became a mantra for Jesus's followers that made their version of messianism distinct from other first-century Jews.

Jesus and the end of days

Not only did Jesus believe in a God of action, not only did he think that the God of Israel would judge the nations, he had an "end of the world" mentality. Some might call this "apocalyptic," but our modern notion of the apocalypse is different than what first-century Jews would have thought of this category. (In Jesus's context, an "apocalypse" was a revealing of some aspect of heavenly reality.) Scholars sometimes use the word "eschatology," meaning the interest in the last things. Jesus, it seems, promoted an eschatology that included a new world order with God as king.

In the first generation after Jesus was gone, his followers were conflicted about what to do with his eschatological perspective. We see evidence of this conflict in the diverse perspectives

---

MEET THIS WORD: ANGEL

Angels are personalities that appear at important moments in the New Testament to deliver messages from heaven. The Greek word *angelos* can refer to human messengers (like John the Baptist), or heavenly messengers (like Gabriel). An angel, in this context, is someone sent by God for this purpose. The European tradition of the word emphasizes the heavenly quality of angels. The Old French *angele* and the Latin *angelus* carry the sense of a heavenly being that serves God.

---

represented in the New Testament writings. Some of these writings suggest that Jesus has ascended to heaven and will return himself as divine judge in short order (before the first generation of disciples has died). Some of these writings suggest a collective worry that Jesus has not returned as soon as expected. So it is clear that some kind of eschatological judgment was expected by both Jesus and the authors of the New Testament. The details of this divine event, however, varies from text to text.

This fact creates a problem for historians who would like to differentiate Jesus's historical teaching on the topic from what the early Church taught after Jesus was gone. *How do we know what Jesus said vs. what his followers said about him?* Take, for example, the following passage (keep in mind that Jesus often refers to himself as the "Son of Man" in the gospels). Here, Jesus is speaking about the signs of the final judgment:

> When he was sitting on the Mount of Olives, the disciples came to him privately, saying, "Tell us, when will this be, and what will be the sign of your coming and of the end of the age?" Jesus answered them, "Beware that no one leads you astray. For many will come in my name, saying, 'I am the Messiah!' and they will lead many astray. And you will hear of wars and rumors of wars; see that you are not alarmed; for this must take place, but the end is not yet." (Matt. 24:3–6)

There are several factors in this passage that lead scholars to believe that this was invented by the early Church and attributed to Jesus – that Jesus never said these words. This would include: (a) Jesus seems to have a royal and almost divine opinion of himself; (b) these instructions seem relevant to an early Christianity under persecution; (c) poor, hungry, imprisoned, naked, and foreign people become representatives of Jesus in this passage. This might suggest that Jesus himself is not there in the flesh to care for anymore. On the other hand, there are a few features of this passage that seem to come from Jesus's historical character; (x) Jesus probably referred to himself as the "Son of Man" and to God as his "Father"; (y) Jesus probably did teach his disciples to care for those in need; (z) Jesus probably did believe in the Devil and predict the Devil's ultimate defeat.

Later in the same passage, Jesus says:

> Immediately after the suffering of those days the sun will be darkened, and the moon will not give its light; the stars will fall from heaven, and the powers of heaven will be shaken. Then the sign of the Son of Man will appear in heaven, and then all the tribes of the earth will mourn, and they will see the Son of Man coming on the clouds of heaven with power and great glory. And he will send out his angels with a loud trumpet call, and they will gather his elect from the four winds, from one end of heaven to the other. (Matt. 24:29–31)

So does this passage reflect the opinions of Jesus about the "last days," or does it reflect the beliefs of the early Church? Or do we see here a combination of both? Perhaps a both/and solution works. Maybe Jesus taught something like this and it was later packaged with language that made sense to the early Church?

In Matthew 24, Jesus is not confident about *when* these end-of-world signs would take place. He says, "But about that day and hour no one knows, neither the angels of heaven, nor the Son, but only the Father" (Matt. 24:36). Ultimately, Jesus could not answer the disciples question about when these things would happen. It is possible that the early Church invented this saying and attributed it to Jesus because they themselves did not know how to answer the question. Conversely, perhaps we have a window into Jesus's own self-conscious limitations. He believed God would act, but he was unable to predict when God would act.

Conclusion

In order to understand Jesus as a historical figure, we must acknowledge that he was preoccupied with what we now call the supernatural. Modern minds tend to separate god-talk from politics, science, and history. But Jesus – alongside many of his contemporaries – interpreted his life, his nation, world events, and the future through a theological filter.

If you asked Jesus about Roman taxes, he might turn the conversation to what is owed to God. If you asked Jesus about illness, he might turn the conversation to the nature of sin. If you asked Jesus about his own authority, he might turn the conversation to demonology.

The same can be said for most of Jesus's first followers. They interpreted Jesus (variously) as a healer, a messiah, a prophet, the Son of God, a heavenly judge, etc. So, while there can be no doubt that Jesus's legacy was shaped by theological categories, we see that Jesus himself contributed to the shaping of his own story.

Five books about Jesus and his historical setting

Bond, H.K. *The Historical Jesus: A Guide for the Perplexed.* (London: T&T Clark, 2012).

Keith, C. *Jesus Against the Scribal Elite.* (Grand Rapids: Baker Academic, 2014).

Levine, A.-J. *Short Stories by Jesus: The Enigmatic Parables of a Controversial Rabbi*. (New York: HarperOne, 2015).

Sanders, E.P. *The Historical Figure of Jesus*. (London: Penguin, 1994).

Schröter, J. *Jesus of Nazareth: Jew from Galilee, Savior of the World*, trans. Wayne Coppins and S. Brian Pounds. (Waco: Baylor University Press, 2014).

2

Jesus in early literature

"Self-perception is only partial perception, and while the passing of time dims memories, it can also unfold significance... The Nazarene never lived solely to himself, never resided exclusively within his own skin. He was always interacting with others, and their perceptions of him must constitute part of his identity, as must his post-Easter influence and significance."

Dale C. Allison, Jr.

Introduction: The storied shape

I begin this section by asking you to use your imagination. I would like you to put yourself in the shoes of a second-generation (still first-century) follower of Jesus. The following sketch is only hypothetical, but perhaps illustrates how Jesus took shape in early Christian literature.

Imagine that you are a Christian living in Rome about forty years after the crucifixion of Jesus. Suppose that you attend a house church near the east market. The small group gathers before sunrise. They sing hymns. They give words to their faith. You repeat the creed with them:

> Christ, born from David's seed, according to the flesh;
> Christ, declared Son of God, according to the spirit.*

You've experienced the Lord Christ in your prayer life. Your entire life has been reoriented around his spiritual presence. But, unlike the elders of your church, you never met Jesus in person. Your father did. Your father once heard Jesus preach in Capernaum. He was devastated by Christ's death and came to believe – as did your whole family – that Christ had risen. Now your father has gone. In fact, most of the generation that had met Jesus in person had passed away. With the passing of that generation, you feel even more distance from Jesus.

In this scenario, we imagine what was probably common among the Christians of the second generation: small gatherings, a few hymns, a heavy reliance on the first generation. We should assume that, at this point in early Christianity, there were no (or very few) written accounts of Jesus's life. There was no "New Testament" to serve as an authoritative framework. A church like the one described here might have had a letter written by Paul (or some other leader), but very few people could tell the whole story of Jesus from personal experience. So most churches relied on the idiosyncratic memories of the first generation.

"I saw Jesus preach in Capernaum."

"I saw him cast out an unclean spirit."

"My mother supported him with food and shelter. She donated money to his group."

"I visited the tomb. Sure enough, it was empty."

Each connection would carry a story with it. What nobody had, however, was a complete picture: a unified and coherent narrative. Worse, some of the personal recollections conflicted.

---

* Here I am paraphrasing Rom. 1:3–4. Many scholars believe that this passage represents an early Christian statement of faith. I will address this passage more fully later.

"I heard him say, 'If you're not with me, you're against me.' "

"No! I was with him when he said, 'If you're not against me, you're with me!' "*

Such debates might be settled by an elder. Leaders possessing the most authority were those who had some person-to-person connection with Jesus. But what happened when these elders started struggling with memory lapses in old age? What if these leaders began to pass away? Or what if one of these churches was established by an eyewitness, but that founding member had relocated?

This would present a number of problems for churches of the second generation. Who will tell the stories about Jesus? Who will settle disputes? How will we know if a new teaching is compatible with the teachings of Jesus? How will we feel connected to Jesus now that the first generation is gone?

Now imagine that a performer, an actor, is in town. He's performing a one-man show called "the Good News." It's a dramatic retelling of Jesus's public life, his wrongful execution, and his resurrection. The performer claims that his story had been approved by the Apostle Peter. If Peter – being the greatest authority on the topic – approved this performance, this story would allow the second generation to experience Jesus in a new and intimate way.

This might be how a shorter narrative like the Gospel of Mark was composed. Perhaps a scribe was employed to write down this performance in service to a church. And once written down, we can imagine that a complete story like this might make a profound difference for a church like the one described earlier. Even though most people in the church could not read the text,

---

* Here I am paraphrasing two verses. Mark 9:40: "Jesus said that 'He who is not against us is for us' "; Luke 11:23: (Jesus said) "He who is not with me is against me."

portions of it could be memorized.* An official document could settle disputes. Most importantly, the physical document (either a papyrus or parchment) would serve as the voice from the first generation; it was a physical connection to Jesus.

This is just an educated guess of how the first narratives of Jesus came to be written down and circulated. But whatever the case, we know that various stories about Jesus coalesced in the form of "gospels" in the second generation.

The title "gospel" derives from a less formal word meaning "good news." For example, we could translate the title attached to Mark's story of Jesus like this:

"The beginning of the *good news* of Jesus Christ, the Son of God."

or

"The beginning of the *gospel* of Jesus Christ, the Son of God."

Used in this way, a gospel is a declaration of good news. If we read further in Mark, we see the word again: "Jesus came to Galilee, proclaiming the good news of God." (Notice that Mark is pointing to Jesus as "Son of God," and Jesus is pointing directly to "God.") Eventually, gospel came to mean, more generally, any composition about Jesus. But at this early stage – so it seems – gospels took the form of biographies.

All of this supposes that the story of Jesus is "good" in some way. So what makes it good? I will suggest three answers:

1. This scenario involving the hypothetical house church in Rome suggests an answer. It is good news because it's a way to experience the Lord Christ, a way to maintain intimacy with those departed, and a way to fortify group identity. It is good news because it helps to solve a crisis of the second generation.

---

* Most people in the first century were illiterate or only able to read and write a few words.

2. The story of Jesus is good because it explains how Jesus – wrongfully executed – was brought back to life. It is the story that the grave could not defeat the Son of God. This key element of theology seems to have been foundational from the very beginning of Christian belief. And if the grave cannot ultimately hold the children of God, the parents, sisters, brothers, and friends of the first generation – those who were dying and who had died – were not gone forever.

3. My third answer reaches back to Jesus himself. Here I assume that Jesus said something akin to what we find in Mark 1:14–15:

> Jesus came to Galilee, proclaiming the good news of God and saying, "The time is fulfilled, and the kingdom of God has come near; repent, and believe in the good news."

These are the first public words of Jesus according to Mark. As such, Mark seems to present this short proclamation as Jesus's primary message. In other words, if Jesus could be reduced to a sound bite for the evening news, this would be it. Jesus seems to be saying (and here I paraphrase), "God will soon rule this world as if God is king." This, of course, would only be "good news" to people who were dissatisfied with the Roman government and hopeful that Jesus's god would be an improvement. Jesus seems to be inviting people to accept a new, divinely established government as good news. So it could be that Jesus was known to have used the phrase: "good news."* If second-generation Christians wanted to feel closer to Jesus, perhaps they repeated some of his better-known phrases. It could be that one of these phrases – "good news" – took the form of a label: a way to encapsulate Jesus's entire story.

---

* Jesus may well have been echoing certain passages from the prophet Isaiah – e.g. Isa. 40:9; 52:7.

I do not think that any single answer needs to be right at the expense of the others. The bottom line is that second-generation Christians thought that having an account of Jesus's public career, his wrongful execution, and ultimate vindication was a good idea.

This development also meant that Jesus – once a dynamic, prophetic voice – had become a character in a story. Jesus would now be encountered in storied shape. This is the fate of all historic figures. They become literary characters.

Furthermore, Jesus was such a compelling literary character that his story attracted prefixes, appendixes, expansions, and redactions. Over the next four centuries, writers fascinated with Jesus would continue to add to this story or rewrite it from scratch. This creative enterprise created a pressure on subsequent generations to decide which stories of Jesus were official and authoritative and useful for the life of the Church. Eventually, mainstream Christianity would limit the official corpus to four first-century narratives: Matthew, Mark, Luke, and John.

Jesus becomes "Jesus"

When did Jesus become Jesus? Jesus and his family likely spoke Aramaic or Hebrew. If so, "Jesus" was not what he was called growing up. His name would have sounded like *Isho* (ee-show). If spoken in Hebrew, his name would have sounded like *Yeshu* (yeh-shoo). Our first evidence for Jesus emerges from a Jewish teacher named Paul who wrote letters in Greek in the mid-first century. During this period, Greek was the most commonly spoken language in the Roman Empire.

After experiencing the resurrected Jesus, Paul (formerly "Saul") believed that God wanted him to spread the good news to non-Jews as well as Jews. In service to this calling, Paul sent letters to many Greek-speaking churches all over the Roman Empire. In a letter to Jesus's followers in Rome, Paul quotes an

---

MEET THIS WORD: CREED

A creed is a succinct statement of belief. Creeds function to make important doctrines official and authoritative, and to unify a worshipping community around a particular theology. In the history of Christianity, creedal statements drew distinctions between groups. Examples include the Nicene Creed and Apostles' Creed (both taking final shape in the fourth century CE).

---

early hymn or creed. This creed is probably our earliest evidence for the life of Jesus. The creed would predate the writing of Paul's letter to Rome (circa 50 CE), and may well emerge from the first generation of Jesus-followers. The creed goes something like this:

> descended from David according to the flesh
>
> declared to be Son of God with power according to the spirit of holiness
>
> by resurrection from the dead, Jesus Christ our Lord (Rom. 1:3–4)

This statement of faith reveals a number of important details about the early (perhaps the earliest) followers of Jesus. First, even though written by Paul in Greek, this statement looks like it first took shape in a Semitic language (i.e. Aramaic or Hebrew). The first two lines appear to be composed in parallel verse, along the lines of Hebrew poetry. Also, the phrase "spirit of holiness" echoes Semitic grammar, rather than the later Christian title "Holy Spirit." But what is even more striking is the phrase "descended from David." This is clearly a reference to the great King David who was anointed with oil by the prophet Samuel in Bethlehem. Thus, even though the earliest known reference to Jesus emerges in Greek, it reveals that the first followers of Jesus were Jewish and well versed in Israelite scripture. Moreover, they probably recited or sang this statement in Aramaic or Hebrew.

Somewhere along the way this creed – built upon Israel's political history – became a common mantra among a subset of Greek-speaking Romans. Both Jews and non-Jews recited this as they worshipped the God of Israel by venerating Jesus as "Lord." One reason that Paul cites this hymn/creed at the beginning of his letter to Rome is to show them that he believes the same thing that they do. It seems that many of Jesus's followers – regardless of geography or ethnicity – embraced Jewish politics by embracing Jesus as Lord.

This creed (at least as Paul frames it) also reveals how many early followers interpreted the resurrection. Jesus, according to Paul, is to be called "Lord." This word could simply mean "master" or "sir," but many Jews used this title to refer to God the Creator. If this is indeed what the term "Lord" means in this context, it reveals that many followers projected divine status onto Jesus at least by the year 50 CE, and perhaps before.

We have no evidence of any resistance to the shift from Semitic languages to Greek. The most likely reason for this is that many people in this context were multilingual. The good news about Jesus's resurrection and God's restoration of David's throne passed seamlessly into the Greek-speaking world. Indeed, this was inevitable as soon as Paul decided to talk about Jesus to non-Jews.

Paul's historical Jesus

The Gospel of Mark is the first narrative of Jesus's life and teachings. This gospel writes of Jesus's political conflicts, death, and resurrection. Mark's gospel, by our best calculations, was composed around 70 CE. But, as discussed earlier, the first writings about Jesus come from a Pharisee named Paul. The Apostle Paul (also called "St Paul") is best known for his letter writing. Some of Paul's letters may even predate Mark by twenty years.

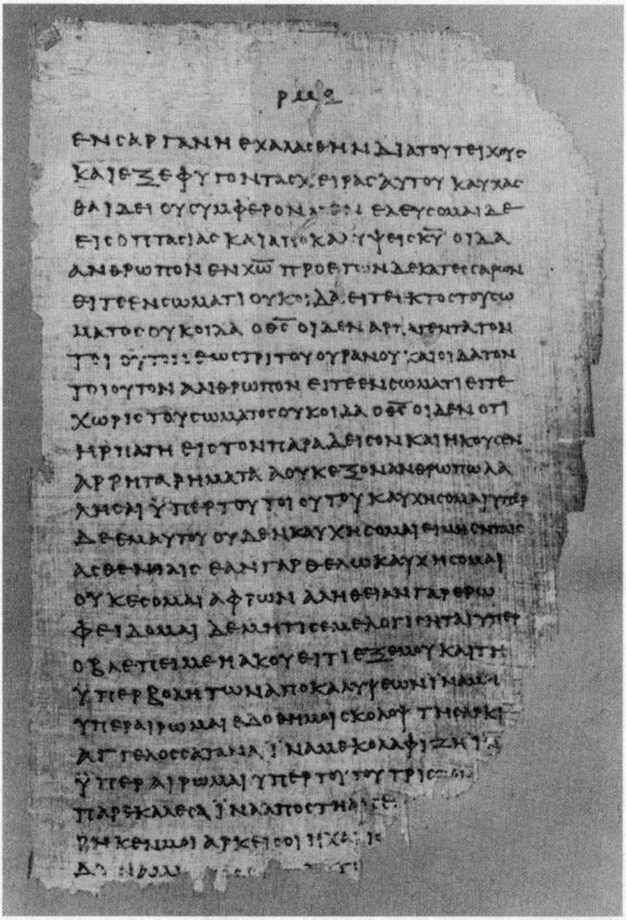

Figure 6 Folio from P46: From Papyrus 46, this is one of the oldest surviving copies of Paul's letters (circa late second century ᴄᴇ). The Greek text corresponds to 2 Cor. 11:33–12:9. There are thirteen letters written under the name "Paul" in the New Testament. Of the thirteen, some may have been written by other early Christians (perhaps using Paul's name after his death). The letters most accepted as genuine are Romans, 1 Corinthians, 2 Corinthians, Galatians, Philippians, 1 Thessalonians, and Philemon.

Paul is preoccupied with the *significance* of Jesus, rather than the stories about his life. Paul's excitement about what Jesus has become in the lives of his followers overshadows almost all else. But although Paul does not say much about Jesus's life, he does say a few interesting things that indicate his general knowledge.

Gleaning from Paul's undisputed letters – the earliest evidence for the life of Jesus – we learn that Jesus's followers believed:

Jesus was "born of a woman" (Gal. 4:4), as a human (Phil. 2:7)

Jesus was Jewish and subject to Jewish law (Gal. 4:4)

Jesus was from the lineage of Abraham (Gal. 3:16) and King David (Rom. 1:3)

Jesus had brothers and they were married men – implying sisters-in-law, nephews, and nieces (1 Cor. 9:5)

Noteworthy among Jesus's brothers is James (Gal. 1:19)

Jesus had a group of disciples called "the twelve" (1 Cor. 15:5)

Noteworthy among these disciples were Peter and John (Gal. 2:9)

Jesus's mission and ministry were primarily to his fellow Jews (Rom. 15:8)

Jesus taught that the practice of food purity is flexible depending on one's point of view (Rom. 14:14)

Jesus gave ethical instructions to his disciples about sexual purity (1 Thess. 4:2–6)

Jesus gave ethical instructions to his disciples about divorce and remarriage (1 Cor. 7:10)

Jesus gave ethical instructions to his disciples about wage-earning for preachers (1 Cor. 9:14)

Jesus was not motivated by his own pleasures (Rom. 15:3) – perhaps suggesting an ethical model of altruism

Jesus instructed his followers to enact a ritual meal in remembrance of him. This meal included bread and wine, and was interpreted by Jesus to represent his body and his blood (1 Cor. 11:23–5)

Jesus was in some way "betrayed" (1 Cor. 11:23)

This betrayal happened at night (1 Cor. 11:23)

Jesus was crucified (1 Cor. 1:23; Phil. 2:8, etc.)

This execution was a public display (Gal. 3:1)

The authorities in Judea are blamed (by Paul) for his death – Paul blames "the Jews/Judeans"* (1 Thess. 2:15)

---

* There is much scholarly debate about whether the Greek word *Ioudaios* should be translated as "Judean" or "Jew." I am sensitive to the concerns of both arguments, but lean toward a both/and solution. It is important that we do not remove references to "the Jews" from the New Testament in a way that whitewashes history. I include this issue of translation here because Paul is clearly referring to a conflict that took place "in Judea" (1 Thess. 2:14). This suggests that he has a regional designation in mind, and some scholars would argue that "Judeans" best captures this. It should also be said that New Testament passages like 1 Thess. 2:14–16 have been used by Christians as a warrant to oppress and murder millions of Jews over the past 2,000 years. Paul, himself a "Hebrew of Hebrews" (as he calls himself), with a deep investment in the well-being of Judea, did not envision such catastrophic violence, and probably never even considered a future version of Christianity devoid of Jewish leadership and hostile to the children of Israel. It also must be said that the Romans (not the Judeans/Jews) were responsible for Jesus's execution. Indeed, I am reluctant to repeat such hateful rhetoric here as it has such a long history of anti-Judaism but there is a danger of erasing "the Jews" from any portion of the New Testament. Attempts to remove

Jesus's crucifixion was a demonstration of his humility (Phil. 2) – perhaps suggesting that Jesus himself was ultimately responsible for his death

Jesus's death was in some way a ritual sacrifice (1 Cor. 5:7) put forth by God (Rom. 3:24–5) – perhaps suggesting that God was ultimately responsible for Jesus's death

Jesus was buried (1 Cor. 15:4)

Jesus was resurrected from the dead "on the third day" (Rom. 1:4; 1 Cor. 15:20, etc.)

In some way, Jesus was raised from death in "fulfillment" of Jewish scriptures (1 Cor. 15:4)*

Jesus appeared to Peter (called Cephas) and then to many other witnesses (1 Cor. 15:5–6)

But if we're hoping for a sketch of historical data, we cannot take such statements at face value. This list cannot be viewed as simple points of fact. Paul, as I have said, is not interested in relaying facts devoid of theological significance. It probably never occurred to Paul to offer an overview of Jesus's life. Paul is a theologian and a rhetorician, not a biographer.

This list is only possible by gleaning the bits and pieces provided by Paul as he quotes early Christian creeds and sayings of Jesus incidentally. Even so, Paul's assumptions of Jesus as a figure in history are helpful as we sketch an image of Jesus's life and impact.

---

references to ancient Jews relate to attempts to physically displace and/or kill contemporary Jews. In this way, the matter of translation is a complex and ethically charged matter.

* What part of Hebrew scripture does Paul have in mind? This question must remain unanswered as there are no predictions of a crucified messiah in the Hebrew scripture, much less a resurrected messiah.

Embracing irony

Jesus was crucified and thus shamed by way of public execution. Any aspirations he may have had about God's rule, rather than Roman rule, was struck down as he was hoisted up. To make their point, Roman soldiers gave him a crown of thorns and mockingly praised him as king.

One would expect that any person who thought that Jesus might be an anointed prophet or king would think differently of Jesus after his humiliating execution. As discussed earlier, that is what crucifixion was for: it ironically "elevated" a person who had aspirations above their social station by nailing and hanging that person on a post. The cross of Jesus was thus a cruel irony.

In Paul's letter to the Philippians (2:5–11), he includes a hymn that was probably sung within the first generation of Jesus's crucifixion:

> Let the same mind be in you that was in Christ Jesus,
> who, though he was in the form of God,
> did not regard equality with God
> as something to be exploited,
> but emptied himself,
> taking the form of a slave,
> being born in human likeness.
> And being found in human form,
> he humbled himself
> and became obedient to the point of death –
> even death on a cross.
>
> Therefore God also highly exalted him
> and gave him the name
> that is above every name,
> so that at the name of Jesus
> every knee should bend,

in heaven and on earth and under the earth,
and every tongue should confess
that Jesus Christ is Lord,
to the glory of God the Father.

Notice at the end of the first stanza that "death on a cross" is considered a form of humiliation. Jesus begins as "the form of God" in this hymn, but refuses any divine agency that he might possess or exploit. Jesus empties himself until he is the form of a slave and mortal. Not only does he willingly die, Jesus dies on a cross. Contrary to the contextual assumption that Jesus exalted himself and thus warranted humiliation, this hymn claims the opposite: Jesus humbled himself and thus warranted exaltation.

The second stanza claims that the name of Jesus brings glory to God and is worthy of worship. Again, this is the opposite of what one would expect of a crucified leader. The folks who sang this hymn embraced Jesus's exaltation. They made the symbol of crucifixion their own, and gave it new meaning. They believed that Rome was wrong about Jesus's motives, but unwittingly right about his exalted status. What Rome meant to say in ironic sarcasm, this hymn claims as divinely endorsed truth: "Jesus Christ is Lord."

Decades after this hymn was composed, the first biography of Jesus's public life plays this irony in a different way. Sometime between 65 and 70 CE, written stories of Jesus's life were taking shape. The Gospel of Mark was composed when Rome and Judea were at war, when Jerusalem was being defended and destroyed. In Mark's gospel, the Roman representative in Judea is Pontius Pilate. Before sending Jesus to the cross, Pilate interrogates him: "You are the king of the Jews?" says Pilate (Mark 15:2). "You say so," replies Jesus. In this story, Jesus refuses to exalt himself. Rather, Pilate does it for him, albeit unwittingly. Immediately after Jesus dies a Roman centurion testifies, "Truly this man was God's son!" Here, Jesus achieves vindication rather than shame from Roman crucifixion (15:39). In a turn of irony, representatives of Rome endorse Jesus in the highest terms.

The first followers of Jesus, therefore, took an ironic device meant to shame them and embraced a double irony: Jesus as both crucified and divine. With this in mind, consider this statement by Jesus in the Gospel of John. "And I, when I am lifted up from the earth, will draw all people to myself." This biography tends to make explicit statements about Jesus in retrospect, whereas the Gospel of Mark might only hint at them. The narrator explains, "He said this to indicate the kind of death he was to die" (John 12:32–3). Somewhere along the way, Jesus's cross became a badge of honor which attracted a following, rather than repelling would-be followers.

The meal of Jesus

Paul's first letter to the Christians of Corinth depicts Jesus in a formal meal setting. We now refer to this meal as the "Last Supper" or the "Eucharist" (meaning thanksgiving), wherein Christians commemorate the body and blood of Christ as they practice *Communion*. Followers of Jesus practiced this ritual meal from a very early stage. Paul writes:

> For I received from the Lord what I also handed on to you, that the Lord Jesus on the night when he was betrayed took a loaf of bread, and when he had given thanks, he broke it and said, "This is my body that is for you. Do this in remembrance of me." In the same way he took the cup also, after supper, saying, "This cup is the new covenant in my blood. Do this, as often as you drink it, in remembrance of me." For as often as you eat this bread and drink the cup, you proclaim the Lord's death until he comes. (1 Cor 11:23–6)

While this quotation is also repeated in the biblical gospels, Paul's short narrative is the earliest surviving mention of these words.* In sum, Jesus – called "Lord" – claims that the bread is his body and the wine is his blood, representing a new covenant. This short narrative suggests that the earliest followers of Jesus enacted a ritual meal in order to remember Jesus's broken body and blood when he was crucified. According to Paul, performing this meal is a proclamation of "the Lord's death."

The fact that Christians commemorated a horrific execution in the form of a meal may seem bizarre to some. This concern is felt in a second-century letter from a Roman official named Pliny the Younger. Pliny reports what he has learned after interrogating Christians. He writes that the Christians confessed their so-called "error":

> they were in the habit of gathering before dawn on a stated day and singing alternately a hymn to Christ as to a god, and that they bound themselves by an oath, not to the commission of any wicked deed… This done, it was their practice, so they said, to separate, and then to meet together again for a meal, which however was of the ordinary kind and quite harmless. (Epp. x. 96/97)

Pliny's reference to an ordinary and harmless meal suggests that certain Romans were concerned that Christians practiced some sort of extraordinary and harmful meal: namely cannibalism. After all, they claimed to be eating the body of another person. These Christians, in pleading their case to Pliny, assuaged his fears and assured him that the meal was quite benign.

It is worth emphasizing that bread and wine were common staples of life. In using mundane elements to represent something sacred, Jesus and his disciples were ensuring a repeated

---

* John does not include this story, but Jesus does refer to himself as the "bread of life" in John 6:35.

Figure 7 *The Communion of the Apostles* (circa 1659): In this oil painting on canvas, Luca Giordano showcases his rapid, fluid, and emotional Baroque-era style. In his interpretation of the Last Supper, the Apostles are haphazard and scattered, implying lack of direction. The artist thus anticipates Jesus's betrayal and passion narrative to follow. Notice also that the Apostles are not reclined while eating. Rather, Jesus stands as a priest administering a sacrament to a kneeling Apostle, mirroring the artist's own religious culture in Italy.

reminder. Remembering Jesus's body and blood became central to the group's shared identity. The bread and wine became keys to unlock the spiritual meaning of Jesus's crucifixion. Clearly this narrative had staying power: it seems to have been practiced by the earliest followers of Jesus, marked them as strange by Roman prosecutors in the years of their obscurity, and has been practiced continually for two millennia.

Jesus and ethical stories

Jesus is widely remembered as a teacher of ethics, and his favorite vehicle for ethical teaching was storytelling. This might tell us something interesting about how Jesus thought about ethics. Stories are open to a variety of interpretations and ethical applications. So it is possible to walk away from a story told by Jesus and apply his insight differently from your neighbor. There are, however, some key themes that seem quite rigid.

In both Jesus's teachings and the teachings of his earliest followers, care for neighbors, strangers, and enemies is fundamental. This aspect of doctrine is borrowed from the Jewish instruction to care for the foreigner. For example, Exod. 22:21 frames the following as a divine mandate: "You shall not wrong or oppress a resident alien, for you were aliens in the land of Egypt." This is only a single example of a repeated instruction in the Hebrew Bible. Jesus extends and interprets this mandate. And as we read in Matthew, Jesus even suggests that failing to do so will result in a curse: "You that are accursed, depart from me into the eternal fire prepared for the devil and his angels" (Matt. 25:41).

MEET THIS WORD: PARABLE

Parable is an umbrella term that covers certain kinds of stories, comparisons, proverbs, and riddles. The term comes from the Greek word *parabole*, which literally means to "cast alongside." In a sense, a parable gives us a parallel way to think about something. For example, Jesus says that the "kingdom of heaven is like a mustard seed" (Matt. 13:31). The idea here is that something magnificent can grow from something small. Parables are generally marked by comparison, but short, memorable bits of wisdom would also be included under this umbrella term. In Matthew, Mark, and Luke, Jesus speaks repeatedly in parables. John's gospel, by contrast, portrays Jesus's speech in long monologues (which would not be considered parables).

One of Jesus's most famous stories was motivated by this topic. Luke 10:25–37 places Jesus in conversation with a legal expert:

> Just then a lawyer stood up to test Jesus. "Teacher," he said, "what must I do to inherit eternal life?" Jesus said to him, "What is written in the law? What do you read there?" The lawyer answered, "You shall love the Lord your God with all your heart, and with all your soul, and with all your strength, and with all your mind; and your neighbor as yourself." And Jesus said to him, "You have given the right answer; do this, and you will live." But wanting to justify himself, he asked Jesus, "And who is my neighbor?" Jesus replied, "A man was going down from Jerusalem to Jericho, and fell into the hands of robbers, who stripped him, beat him, and went away, leaving him half dead. Now by chance a priest was going down that road; and when he saw him, he passed by on the other side. So likewise a Levite, when he came to the place and saw him, passed by on the other side. But a Samaritan while travelling came near him; and when he saw him, he was moved with pity. He went to him and bandaged his wounds, having poured oil and wine on them. Then he put him on his own animal, brought him to an inn, and took care of him. The next day he took out two denarii, gave them to the innkeeper, and said, 'Take care of him; and when I come back, I will repay you whatever more you spend.' Which of these three, do you think, was a neighbor to the man who fell into the hands of the robbers?" The lawyer said, "The one who showed him mercy." Jesus said to him, "Go and do likewise."

As is typical in the gospels, Jesus is showcased as a rhetorical genius who never loses a debate. In this context, the legal expert is a typical literary feature. He functions literarily to showcase Jesus's rhetorical skill. In reality, such debates are usually very lengthy and are rarely settled by a single parable. Even so, this short passage reveals a crucial characteristic of Jesus and the impact he had on early Christianity. Not only is care for the stranger central to Jesus's preaching, it is central to the way Jesus thinks about salvation. As Luke presents him, Jesus tells this story in direct response to the questions "What must I do to inherit eternal life?" and "Who is my neighbor?"

The first of these questions is met with Jesus's question: "What is written in the law? What do you read there?" Here, Jesus reinforces the value of Jewish legal instruction for his followers. He also suggests that *how one reads the law* is as important as what the law says. In the above passage, Jesus's words are translated as, "What do you read there?" But closer to the Greek would be something like, "How do you read?" This is a conversation over *how* one reads legal instructions. The legal expert, according to Jesus, is right to focus on this passage, "You shall love the Lord your God with all your heart, and with all your soul, and with all your strength, and with all your mind; and your neighbor as yourself."

Now we come to a most surprising element of Jesus's teaching. Jesus is asked, "And who is my neighbor?" But the parable that follows refuses to answer this question. Rather, Jesus explains what it means to be a good neighbor. In effect, Jesus answers the question "Who is my neighbor" by asking, "To whom have you shown mercy?" The implication here is that followers of Jesus must ask themselves a better question: "Am I the neighbor?" Here comes the hard part: according to Jesus, salvation hinges on the way that this question is answered.

Jesus in Mark

The Gospel of Mark is our earliest surviving narrative about Jesus. It focuses exclusively on Jesus's public career, beginning with John the Baptist (and Jesus's baptism), and ending with the empty tomb (pointing to Jesus's resurrection). Mark's story – probably because it is earliest – is often treated as the most "authentic" representation of Jesus's life. It must be said, however, that Mark wrote in Greek and looks to have been writing for a largely non-Jewish audience. So Mark is distanced from Jesus in both language and cultural framing. (Each of the four biblical gospels were written in Greek.) The author of Mark may have been alive before Jesus died, but the text makes no claim of this. Still, Mark probably gives an impression of Jesus's public career that seemed plausible to those familiar with his public life. Moreover, this is as much as we can hope from any ancient biographical portrait.

Mark's account is only sixteen short chapters. Each chapter is only a page or two in length, and it takes less than one and a half hours to read his entire narrative. It is likely that it was composed to be performed orally. Most scholars date its composition to around 70 CE.

MEET THIS WORD: SATAN

The Hebrew word *satan* did not originate as a proper name. The term is used for characters who (whether for good or bad) act adversarially. For example, Num. 22:32 depicts an angel who blocks Balaam's path, saying, "Behold, I have come out as an adversary [*satan*], because your way was contrary to me." In this story, the angel is called the "Angel of the Lord." The term is eventually personified in Jewish literature as a specific character who opposes God and Israel (Job 1:6–12). In Mark 8:33, Jesus rebukes Peter by calling him a "satan." It is unclear if Jesus means to associate Peter with the literary character, or if he merely means that Peter is acting adversarially.

Mark's Jesus preaches about the kingdom (or rule) of God. In Mark, Jesus speaks in short parables and is often argumentative. He elevates simple questions into bold assertions. He changes the subject often when arguing so that he can outwit people. He also rebukes his disciples and other Jewish leaders. In one story he calls Peter a "satan" (Mark 8:33). In another story, he compares a Syrophoenician woman – perhaps her entire people – to dogs (Mark 7:24–7). In short, Jesus is the type of person who picks verbal fights. One wonders if this is part of the reason Jesus found himself in trouble with Jerusalem's leadership and (ultimately) in trouble with Rome.

On the other hand, Mark's Jesus is a man who reaches out to children, lepers, and other people without social standing. Jesus generally visits villages and people in rural areas, and does not often go to cities to preach in marketplaces. Mark's Jesus is generally combative against those with social power and generous to those without it.

A key plot point in Mark is that Jesus is wildly popular with people who want healing or who are tormented by demons. Add to this Jesus's reputation as a storyteller and preacher, and it is easy to see why people flocked to him.

> Again he began to teach beside the lake. Such a very large crowd gathered around him that he got into a boat on the lake and sat there, while the whole crowd was beside the lake on the land. He began to teach them many things in parables. (Mark 4:1)

Mark repeatedly includes details about the numbers of people thronging to him. This passage also mentions the creative solution to use the water as a natural amphitheater to create a stage. Literally speaking, the stage was a boat.

Sometimes we get the sense that Jesus would rather be solitary but that the crowds seek him out anyway. Consider also the way the crowd functions as a single entity to drive the plot in this story:

> On that day, when evening had come, he said to them, "Let us go across to the other side." And *leaving the crowd behind*, they took him with them in the boat, just as he was. Other boats were with him. A great gale arose, and the waves beat into the boat, so that the boat was already being swamped. But he was in the stern, asleep on the cushion; and they woke him up and said to him, "Teacher, do you not care that we are perishing?" He woke up and rebuked the wind, and said to the sea, "Peace! Be still!" Then the wind ceased, and

Figure 8 A first-century Galilean boat: The remains were discovered in the mud of the Sea of Galilee. While it is sometimes called the "Jesus boat," it has no formal connection to Jesus. It is possible, however, that he once sat in a boat like this. It is displayed at the Yigal Allon Museum in Kibbutz Ginosar.

there was a dead calm. He said to them, "Why are you afraid? Have you still no faith?" And they were filled with great awe and said to one another, "Who then is this, that even the wind and the sea obey him?" (Mark 4:35–41)

The story suggests that Jesus was finished with the crowds and so boarded the boat to leave them behind. But, of course, this problem drives the plot further in that something important about Jesus's character is revealed: he as an agent of God who is able to speak with the voice of God. Indeed, who else can tame the chaos of the storm? Mark plays with a key theme in Jewish scripture: the voice of God brings order amidst chaos.

The crowds are an important feature of Mark's narrative. They serve to create a sense of Jesus's popularity, but they will eventually dissipate and then reconvene to shout, "Crucify him!" In a sense, Jesus ultimately succumbs to the storm; but it will be the stormy gales of politics that drown him.

Mark's Jesus is also notable for what the story does not include. For example, Mark does not tell any stories of Jesus's birth or childhood. Mark never mentions his father, Joseph. Mark does not preserve many of Jesus's sayings that are found in the other gospels. Mark is also without an extended account of Jesus's resurrection appearances. The earliest manuscripts simply end with an interpretation of Jesus's empty tomb. But even if read without Jesus's appearances, the story ends with an assurance of the risen Jesus. Indeed, this is what the empty tomb means. Mark depicts women who encounter an (angelic) man at the tomb:

> As they entered the tomb, they saw a young man, dressed in a white robe, sitting on the right side; and they were alarmed. But he said to them, 'Do not be alarmed; you are looking for Jesus of Nazareth, who was crucified. He has been raised; he is not here. Look, there is the place they laid him. (Mark 16:5–6)

Perhaps the most prominent theme in Mark – indeed the one that drives the narrative – is Jesus's innocence and ultimate vindication. Jesus's public shaming and execution would have proven to many that he was not endorsed by God. Mark's story refutes this logic by showing that Jesus was indeed divinely endorsed. Jesus may have been tried and executed, but he was ultimately vindicated. This might explain why almost half of Mark is devoted to Jesus's final week (what we call the "Passion narrative") and the events leading to his crucifixion. Mark puts forth a Jesus who was indeed God's agent, although misunderstood and wrongfully put to death.

Jesus in Matthew

The Gospel of Matthew was believed by some early Christians to have been the first written. The scholarly consensus now assumes that both Matthew and Luke (and possibly John) borrow from and expand Mark's story. The author/editor of Matthew may well have enhanced Mark with other well-known stories about Jesus, and thereby "corrected" Mark's omissions. It is highly unlikely that this author/editor believed that such enhancement did damage to a previously pure tradition. It is much more likely that Matthew wanted to clarify and expound details that Mark has underplayed.

For example, in Mark, Jesus is called the Messiah. Matthew agrees and includes further proof and explanation. To this end, Matthew cites Hebrew scripture and claims that many prophecies have been fulfilled by Jesus; he connects Jesus to the great kings David and Solomon; and he also portrays Jesus as a new Moses. These are just three examples of concepts introduced by Mark and then developed as larger themes in Matthew.

In addition to enhancing or correcting Mark's story, Matthew also adds new material. Most of this material is in the form of short sayings attributed to Jesus. One example of this is Jesus's most famous ethical statement – the "Sermon on the Mount":

> When Jesus saw the crowds, he went up the mountain; and after he sat down, his disciples came to him. Then he began to speak, and taught them, saying:
>
> "Blessed are the poor in spirit, for theirs is the kingdom of heaven. Blessed are those who mourn, for they will be comforted.
> Blessed are the meek, for they will inherit the earth.
> Blessed are those who hunger and thirst for righteousness, for they will be filled.
> Blessed are the merciful, for they will receive mercy.

Blessed are the pure in heart, for they will see God.

Blessed are the peacemakers, for they will be called children of God.

Blessed are those who are persecuted for righteousness' sake, for theirs is the kingdom of heaven.

Blessed are you when people revile you and persecute you and utter all kinds of evil against you falsely on my account.

Rejoice and be glad, for your reward is great in heaven, for in the same way they persecuted the prophets who were before you." (Matt. 5:1–12)

In this first part of the sermon, which is also called the "Beatitudes," we see a few of Matthew's key interests. Matthew's Jesus begins with ten instructions for his followers, given from a mountain,

Figure 9 *The Sermon on the Mount* by Károly Ferenczy (1896): This oil painting on canvas contains elements of the artistic theme of naturalism. The artist may be expressing the superiority of undeterred nature over humankind and, in this case, religion. Ferenczy could also be observing the incongruity between Jesus's teaching and institutional Christianity, underscored by the anachronistic attire of the reclining figures and the awkward foreground.

which echoes the Hebrew tradition of Moses who receives the Ten Commandments on a mountain.

In this sermon, Jesus also seems to be drawing from and reframing the idea of blessing. In the Hebrew scriptures, to be blessed often meant to be filled with life potency (e.g. fertile) or to be victorious (e.g. in war). It is interesting, then, to see how Matthew's Jesus reframes the concept. That said, many of the themes found here echo a genre of Hebrew writing called "wisdom literature": the virtue of mourning (Eccl. 7:2–4), righteousness (Prov. 20:7), mercy (Ps. 85:10), purity in heart (Prov. 22:11), and peace (Ps. 34:14).

In the above sermon, Matthew's Jesus twice refers to the "kingdom of heaven," whereas Mark's Jesus prefers the phrase "kingdom of God." It could be that Matthew has developed a tendency to write "heaven" instead of "God" out of reverence for God. If so, "heaven" is just another way to say "God." But Matthew does use the term "God" as well in this sermon. Whatever the case, first-century Jews did not have the same concept of heaven as modern people do.* Jesus was probably not referring to a place where people go after death. It is more likely that Matthew's Jesus is concerned with the ethics of everyday life, which carry risks and rewards in the real world.

---

* There were probably many different ways that Jesus's Jewish contemporaries thought about the afterlife. Some believed in the resurrection of the physical body during God's final judgment. Some might have believed that death was simply the end: for instance, the author of Ecclesiastes writes: "But whoever is joined with all the living has hope, for a living dog is better than a dead lion. The living know that they will die, but the dead know nothing; they have no more reward, and even the memory of them is lost. Their love and their hate and their envy have already perished; never again will they have any share in all that happens under the sun" (Eccl. 9:4–6).

Finally, Matthew differs from Mark in that Jesus's public career is exclusively meant for the people of Israel. Indeed he specifically tells his disciples, "Go nowhere among the Gentiles and enter no town of the Samaritans, but go rather to the lost sheep of the house of Israel" (Matt. 10:5–6). It isn't until the very end of Matthew that Jesus says, "Therefore go and make disciples of all nations" (28:19). Matthew's Jesus is focused exclusively on his fellow Jews; but just before he departs, he commands his followers to broaden the scope of their mission.

Unfortunately Matthew's portrait of Jesus also heightens his criticism of other Jewish leaders. Matthew's Jesus is especially damning of the Pharisees, scribes, and priests. Matthew also stresses Judas's collaboration with "Caiaphas," the high priest named by Matthew to arrest Jesus. Matthew's story of Jesus has had a tragic impact on Jewish-Christian relations. Matthew expands and embellishes Jesus's vitriol for his countrymen. This rhetoric was repeated over and over again throughout the history of Christianity to justify violence against Jews and Judaism. For this reason, many scholars consider Matthew to have an anti-Jewish agenda.*

On the other hand, we find a deep contradiction in Matthew because he spotlights a Jesus who refers to Jewish patriarchs, stories and purity. Indeed, Matthew's Jesus says:

> Do not think that I have come to abolish the law or the prophets; I have come not to abolish but to fulfill. For truly I tell you, until heaven and earth pass away, not one letter, not one stroke of a letter, will pass from the law until all is accomplished. Therefore, whoever breaks one of the least of these commandments, and teaches others to do the same, will be called least in the kingdom of heaven; but whoever does them and teaches them will be called great in the kingdom of heaven. (Matt. 5:17–19)

---

* See especially Matthew 23.

Clearly Matthew's Jesus is recognizably Jewish and even portrayed as someone who is even more observant than his fellow countrymen. It is then lamentable that Matthew's portrait has been used to the detriment of Jews and Judaism throughout history.

Jesus in Luke

The Gospel of Luke generally follows Mark's story (chronology, plot, key characters) while also extending Mark's effort to make Jesus intelligible to a non-Jewish audience. Again – as with all four biblical gospels – Luke presents Jesus in a story written in Greek. Luke is especially interested in people who are of lower social standing.

Luke emphasizes the testimonies of women connected to Jesus, including stories about Mary (Jesus's mother) and Elizabeth (Mary's older relative). And both women sing songs that foreshadow things to come. While Jesus is in her womb, Mary sings:

> My soul glorifies the Lord and my spirit rejoices in God my Savior, for he has been mindful of the humble state of his servant. From now on all generations will call me blessed, for the Mighty One has done great things for me – holy is his name. His mercy extends to those who fear him, from generation to generation. He has performed mighty deeds with his arm; he has scattered those who are proud in their inmost thoughts. He has brought down rulers from their thrones but has lifted up the humble. He has filled the hungry with good things but has sent the rich away empty. He has helped his servant Israel, remembering to be merciful to Abraham and his descendants forever, just as he promised our ancestors. (Luke 1:46–55)

In this song, Mary represents a key theme in Luke. She sings of the reversal of fortunes: the proud are scattered; rulers are ousted; the rich are emptied. Conversely, the humble are elevated. This foreshadows one of Jesus's agendas in the story: care for the poor and indictment of the wealthy. Consider Luke's version of the Sermon on the Mount (in Luke it takes place on a plain, not a mountain):

Then he looked up at his disciples and said:

"Blessed are you who are poor, for yours is the kingdom of God.
Blessed are you who are hungry now, for you will be filled.
Blessed are you who weep now, for you will laugh.
Blessed are you when people hate you, and when they exclude you, revile you, and defame you on account of the Son of Man.
Rejoice on that day and leap for joy, for surely your reward is great in heaven; for that is what their ancestors did to the prophets.
But woe to you who are rich, for you have received your consolation.
Woe to you who are full now, for you will be hungry.
Woe to you who are laughing now, for you will mourn and weep.
Woe to you when all speak well of you, for that is what their ancestors did to the false prophets." (Luke 6:20–6)

You will notice several parallel statements to Matthew's "Sermon on the Mount." But notice also that the blessings are followed by a series of curses. The idea that the rich/comfortable and the poor/distraught will experience a role reversal is important to Jesus. It becomes a key feature of his parables too.

Another key element of Luke's portrait of Jesus is his relationship to the "Holy Spirit." Luke gives the impression that Jesus is motivated by the Holy Spirit to begin his public ministry, and led into the wilderness to be tempted by the Devil. Jesus resists these temptations, seemingly supercharged by the Holy Spirit; Jesus is "filled with the power of the Spirit" (4:14). In his hometown synagogue, Jesus proclaims (while reading Isaiah): "The Spirit of the Lord is upon me, because he has anointed me to bring good news to the poor" (4:18). Thus the Lukan Jesus is motivated, directed, and enabled to do remarkable things by the special presence of the Lord. Luke refers to the "Holy Spirit" more often than the other gospels, and extends this as a key theme in the sequel to this gospel – the Book of Acts.

Jesus in John

The Gospel of John begins poetically with the idea of "Logos" (this Greek word is sometimes translated as Word, or Wisdom). Jesus, as Logos, is portrayed as a divine agent who existed at the very beginning of time. This is how John starts:

> In the beginning was the Word [Logos], and the Word was with God, and the Word was God. He was in the beginning with God. All things came into being through him, and without him not one thing came into being. What has come into being in him was life, and the life was the light of all people. The light shines in the darkness, and the darkness did not overcome it. (John 1:1–5)*

This portrait of Jesus begins by claiming that the Word [meaning Jesus] "was God" and assisted somehow in God's creation of "all things." This is bold and elevated speech. It might seem commonplace to Christians, but it was a remarkable thing to say about a man best known for his crucifixion in the first century. Thus John explicitly sets Jesus over and against his contemporaries at the start. In this telling of Jesus's life, there is a dividing line between those who understand Jesus's divinity, and those who do not. According to John, the Word "was in the world, and the world came into being through him; yet the world did not know him. He came to what was his own, and his own people did not accept him" (1:10–11). This stark contrast between those

---

* Reading on, it becomes clear that the "Word" is a flesh and blood human named Jesus: "And the Word became flesh and lived among us, and we have seen his glory, the glory as of a father's only son, full of grace and truth. (John testified to him and cried out, 'This was he of whom I said, 'He who comes after me ranks ahead of me because he was before me.' "). From his fullness we have all received, grace upon grace. The law indeed was given through Moses; grace and truth came through Jesus Christ" (John 1:14–17).

who "see the light" and those who live "in darkness" creates a good guy/bad guy scenario in John. The "Jews" in John (a group portrayed as a general stereotype) are painted negatively in large part.*

John's Jesus is probably framed within the Jewish category of "Wisdom personified." Imagine that the concept of wisdom was represented by a singular voice with a distinct personality. In Hebrew wisdom literature, this character is sometimes cast as God's companion: "Lady Wisdom" (compare Proverbs 8). In parallel to Lady Wisdom, Jesus as the "Word" is said to exist with God before creations where he served as a mediating creative force: "All things came into being through him, and without him not one thing came into being" (John 1:2). Elsewhere in John's story, Jesus is depicted with Creator-like powers. Jesus has power over the laws of nature and gives life to the dead (John 6:16–21; 11:38–44). Jesus performs "signs" (what we might think of as miracles) meant to make people believe (e.g. John 2:1–11). And Jesus teaches the truth, demonstrating the path of wisdom (e.g. John 8:32). Along these lines, blindness and sight are also key themes in John's gospel (e.g. John 9).

In addition to these binary themes that draw stark contrasts, John also provides creative commentaries on Jewish tradition. Holidays and feasts are highlighted and used to reveal Jesus's divinity. Because of this, meals become a key element of John's narrative. The Wedding at Cana signals the start of Jesus's public career (2:1–12). Only in John does Jesus turn water into wine. Only in John do we read Jesus's famous "I am the bread of life" discourse (6:22–65). Jesus often travels and celebrates Jewish feast days. After his resurrection, Jesus eats with his disciples (21:12–15). Taken together, it is clear that John is keenly interested in symbols – so much so, that we could say that John is a biography of Jesus framed in highly symbolic language.

---

* Compare, e.g. John 8 with special attention to John 8:44.

Figure 10 *Wedding at Cana* (circa 1308 CE): This tempera painting on wood by Duccio di Buoninsegna shows a young Jesus pouring wine from water jars (see John 2). Duccio builds from a rigid Byzantine foundation, but adds lifelike expression to his work. This influenced much of the art emerging from Siena, Tuscany, during this period.

John also includes several characters that we meet only in this gospel. Multiple times the narrator refers to the "disciple whom Jesus loved" (e.g. 13:23–5; 19:26–7; 20:2–10). It could be that the narrator is using this as a self-referent. If so, this beloved disciple is the author who has written himself into the narrative. The disciple named Nathaniel is also mentioned only in John (1:47). John is the only gospel to include Jesus's conversation with Nicodemus (2:23–3:21). This last conversation is where we read one of Jesus's most famous sayings:

> For God so loved the world that he gave his only Son, so that everyone who believes in him may not perish but may have eternal life. Indeed, God did not send the Son into the world to condemn the world, but in order that the world might be saved through him. (John 3:16)

John's Jesus often calls attention to himself with "I am" statements: "I am the bread of life" (6:48); "I am the light of the world" (8:12); "I say to you, I am the door of the sheep" (10:7); "I am the good shepherd. The good shepherd lays down his life for the sheep" (10:11); "I am the resurrection and the life; he who believes in me, though he die, yet shall he live" (11:25); "I am the way, and the truth, and the life; no one comes to the Father, but by me" (14:6); "I am the true vine, and my Father is the vinedresser" (15:1). It has sometimes been said that the Synoptic Jesus points to the kingdom of God whereas John's Jesus points to himself.

The Synoptic Jesus vs. John's Jesus

Matthew, Mark, and Luke are called the Synoptic Gospels. Synoptic means "seen together" or "affording a general view." Reading these gospels side by side will demonstrate why scholars think they are in the same family of texts: they are alike (for the most part) in chronology, plot, and key elements, and they also duplicate sayings. The scholarly consensus is that these gospels have a literary relationship of some kind. Perhaps Matthew and Luke did not know of each other, but independently copied from Mark's pre-existing gospel. Or perhaps Matthew copied from Mark and then Luke synthesized both. Whatever the case, most scholars are convinced that these gospels are connected in some

Figure 11 *Book of Kells* (circa 800 CE): This folio is an example of "illumination" in Christian art. This particular illumination adorns a book containing the four gospels: Matthew, Mark, Luke, and John. Each gospel writer is assigned a symbol in medieval art: Matthew is the man; Mark is the lion; Luke is the ox; John is the eagle.

way. Indeed, about 90 percent of Mark's story is reproduced in the other two.

The Gospel of John, on the other hand, appears different than the first three in chronology, wording, key elements, etc. I have already listed several of these differences. But it is necessary to say that all four gospels are much more alike than they are dissimilar. They all connect Jesus to John the Baptist, portray him as a Jewish teacher, preacher, debater, healer, and critic of the Jerusalem leadership. All four gospels quote, allude to, and echo Hebrew scripture. In all four gospels, Jesus establishes a following of disciples, is betrayed by one of his own, sentenced to death by Pontius Pilate, crucified, and resurrected.

Here are just a few examples of how John is different from the Synoptic Gospels (Matthew, Mark and Luke). John's Jesus is not an exorcist. While this is a key element in the Synoptics, John never portrays an exorcism. The Gospel of John has no account of Jesus's baptism by John the Baptist, no wilderness temptation by the Devil, no beatitudes, no "Lord's Prayer," and no story of Jesus's ascension to heaven. In John, Jesus rarely uses the phrase "kingdom of God/heaven," whereas this is his central message in the Synoptics. John's chronology of events in the life of Jesus are also different. For example, Jesus enacts his protest in the Temple precincts at the beginning of the story, rather than during his final week as portrayed in Matthew, Mark, and Luke. Also, Jesus travels to Jerusalem multiple times in John, whereas, in the Synoptics, Jesus only visits Jerusalem once. In John, Jesus imparts the Spirit to his disciples by breathing on them.

Tatian's *Diatessaron*

Matthew, Mark, Luke, and John are placed side-by-side in the Christian Bible. But this was not always so. Before there was an official canon of Christian scripture, different house churches made do with whatever was accessible to them. In the second century, very few people had copies of all four gospels. Tatian of Adiabene was an exception. He compared the four-fold tradition and created a single story of Jesus from these gospels.

This single harmony of Matthew, Mark, Luke, and John is known as the *Diatessaron*. The name, in Greek, means "by way of four." Some suggest it was composed around 170 CE in Syria, although an exact date is difficult to nail down. Most of this composite portrait is made up of exact phrases from the four-fold tradition.

Tatian's idea seems simple enough: Why do we need four overlapping, mostly redundant stories about Jesus? Wouldn't it be better to have one official gospel? There are two major problems – we now know – with harmonizing the gospels.

First, the gospels do not always agree on the details. Should we place Jesus's table-turning incident at the beginning (John), or at the end (the Synoptics)? Which list of twelve disciples do we use? What are the exact words inscribed above Jesus's cross? How many people witnessed the empty tomb, who were they, and in what order? Tatian decided to use the Gospel of John as his framework and generally followed John's chronology (Matthew is sometimes favored too). But to smooth out the discrepancies and contradictions between the four gospels, he left about 20 percent of the material out.

Second, there was a widespread desire among the so-called "Apostolic Church" to preserve the witness of the Apostles. An Apostle was someone commissioned by Jesus himself, or who had special leadership status within early Christianity. Having an official document attributed to Peter (which many supposed of Mark), or John (who many supposed to be the disciple), was attractive because it meant that the reader was only a step removed from Jesus himself. In this way, Jesus Christ was encountered through those he personally knew and personally instructed to preach. From this perspective, reworking the earliest stories of Jesus into an amalgam was unattractive. An official gospel needed to have the name of a famous leader from the first generation to lend it authority.

MEET THIS WORD: APOSTOLIC

Apostolic is an adjective that relates to Jesus's Apostles (usually a term reserved for Jesus's twelve disciples). The Greek word *apostolos* refers to a delegate or someone who is sent on a mission. In Christianity, the idea of apostolic succession is important to maintain a link with the teachings passed down from the official disciples of Jesus. In fact, this was a key criterion for determining which gospels were included in the Bible. Books without a strong claim to Apostolic witness were usually set aside. Books written in later centuries, like the gospels of Judas, Mary, and Gamaliel were not thought to have originated from the Apostles of the first century.

Even so, the *Diatesseron* was viewed as authoritative and remained popular in the Syriac Church until the fifth century. Eventually, the four-fold gospel tradition was included in their distinct forms in the Christian canon. In the early history of the Church, Christian authors would simply quote Matthew most of the time.

While his harmonizing effort eventually fell into obscurity, we witness an important development with Tatian. Somebody – perhaps for the first time – noticed that the Apostolic forbears produced four *different* portraits of Jesus that could be compared and contrasted. Crucially, Tatian also demonstrates that the story of Jesus is too big for any single gospel to tell. What Tatian failed to do was to preserve these distinctions as separate narratives. In choosing against the *Diatesseron*, the Church embraced multiple faces of Jesus, rather than one official portrait.

The Gospel of Thomas

The Gospel of Thomas purports to be written by a disciple of Jesus named Didymos Judas Thomas. This composition confounds what we might think of as a "gospel." It is a collection of 114 sayings attributed to Jesus, and contains little narrative. Most notably, it isn't about Jesus's passion, crucifixion, and resurrection. In short, it cannot be classified as a biography of Jesus's public career. But if we think of a gospel as a unit of literature about Jesus, the Gospel of Thomas would seem to fit.

What sort of Jesus do we meet in this gospel? The first two lines of the document give us some clues. I have included below the prefixed title and first saying:*

> These are the secret sayings which the living Jesus spoke and which Didymos Judas Thomas wrote down.

> And he said, "Whoever finds the interpretation of these sayings will not experience death."

The first clue here is the word "secret." Jesus is supposed to have given certain – his most important – teachings in secret. His most important sayings are not for everyone. Moreover, if you are a Christian living in the second century, and you encounter these sayings, you should not be surprised that you'd never heard them before: they were first communicated in secret. Thus, they were not widely circulated.

The second clue is the phrase, "Whoever finds the interpretation." Jesus's opening line indicates that his sayings will require interpretation. So even if you happen to overhear one of his secret teachings, don't expect to understand it. This hidden wisdom requires searching and finding.

There are a few sayings that overlap with what we find in the Synoptic Gospels. There are also a few key themes that overlap: talk of the "kingdom," farming metaphors, negative rhetoric about the Pharisees, etc. In the Gospel of Thomas, Jesus is fond of the phrase, "Whoever has ears to hear, let him hear." This phrase

---

* All quotations from the Gospel of Thomas are from the Thomas O. Lambdin translation. For public use, see:
http://www.earlychristianwritings.com/text/thomas-lambdin.html

is reminiscent of Jesus's saying in Mark 4:9: "Let anyone with ears to hear listen!" Jesus, in verse 26, says: "You see the mote in your brother's eye, but you do not see the beam in your own eye. When you cast the beam out of your own eye, then you will see clearly to cast the mote from your brother's eye." This saying is reminiscent of Matt. 7:3: "Why do you look at the speck of sawdust in your brother's eye and pay no attention to the plank in your own eye?" But Thomas connects this eye metaphor with a unique saying: "Jesus said, 'Love your brother like your soul, guard him like the pupil of your eye' " (25).

True to the secretive intentions of the Gospel of Thomas, some of Jesus's sayings are difficult to understand, and some are baffling. Sayings 109–112 are good examples:

> (109) Jesus said, "The kingdom is like a man who had a hidden treasure in his field without knowing it. And after he died, he left it to his son. The son did not know (about the treasure). He inherited the field and sold it. And the one who bought it went plowing and found the treasure. He began to lend money at interest to whomever he wished."
>
> (110) Jesus said, "Whoever finds the world and becomes rich, let him renounce the world."
>
> (111) Jesus said, "The heavens and the earth will be rolled up in your presence. And the one who lives from the living one will not see death." Does not Jesus say, "Whoever finds himself is superior to the world?"
>
> (112) Jesus said, "Woe to the flesh that depends on the soul; woe to the soul that depends on the flesh."

Saying 109 is difficult to interpret. Is Jesus suggesting that the kingdom is found by luck? Or that some people will have their ignorance held against them? Perhaps these are the natural by-products of secret knowledge: most simply will pass it by. Saying 110 suggests that "finding the world" might bring wealth, but that worldly wealth should be renounced. This would seem to fit with what Jesus teaches about money elsewhere. But "the world" is cast in entirely negative terms, perhaps suggesting that an entirely spiritual existence might be better. Saying 111 would seem to cohere with this reading: he who "finds himself" stands over and against the world, which is temporal. Saying 112 explicitly denounces a dependent relationship between flesh and soul. This saying nods toward a growing Christian belief that the material world is evil, created by an evil deity whereas those with purity of spirit, and who acquire the right knowledge, can transcend the material world.

The idea that the physical world is inferior (or evil) probably reflects the beliefs of the sect that produced this collection. It does not seem to have roots in the teachings of Jesus. However, it is possible that a "core" of Jesus's sayings is preserved in the Gospel of Thomas. Some have argued that it contains an early selection of teachings that snowballed into the second century. Like a snowball, it accumulated more and more sayings along the way. Others argue that it is the product of later Christianity that adapted elements from earlier gospels.

Ignatius: Jesus the paradox

Ignatius of Antioch was a contemporary of the authors of the New Testament. The dates of his life are debatable, but he was probably born in the mid-30s CE and died in the early second century. It is possible that he was a student of John (the Apostle). If so, he was a disciple of a disciple of Jesus.

MEET THIS WORD: FLESH

Literally speaking, flesh is the soft tissue just below the skin of an animal. For many early Christians, it was also an important theological word. In Greek, the word for flesh is *sarx*, and it can simply

MEET THIS WORD: FLESH (cont.)

mean the physicality of the human body. For example, John 1:14 claims the 'Word' became flesh and dwelt among us." Other authors refer to flesh as something that is opposed to the spirit: "what the flesh desires is opposed to the Spirit, and what the Spirit desires is opposed to the flesh; for these are opposed to each other, to prevent you from doing what you want" (Gal. 5:17). In this second sense, flesh is the part of the human psyche that leads us into error. So sometimes *sarx* can be virtuous, sometimes sinful.

Ignatius wrote several letters, none of which are included in the New Testament. In his letter to the Ephesians, he offers a metaphor for understanding Jesus's significance. Ignatius is worried that the Church in Ephesus will slip into false teaching about Jesus, and he instructs the Church to avoid those who tempt them to do so:

> Now Onesimus himself highly praises your orderly conduct in God, reporting that no faction has found a home among you. Indeed, you do not so much as listen to anyone unless he speaks truthfully about Jesus Christ. For there are some who maliciously and deceitfully are accustomed to carrying about the name [of Jesus] while doing other things unworthy of God. You must avoid them as wild beasts. For they are mad dogs that bite by stealth. You must be on your guard against them, for their bite is hard to heal. There is only one physician, who is both flesh and spirit, born and unborn, God in man, true life in death, from both Mary and from God, first subject to suffering and then beyond it, Jesus Christ our Lord. (6.2–7.2)

Ignatius uses the metaphor of Christ the "physician." Here, the metaphor creates a contrast: the correct teachings of Jesus heal, whereas false teachings wound. Given that Jesus was reputed as a faith healer, this seems a fitting extension of his reputation.

What comes next is surprising: "both flesh and spirit, born and unborn, God in man, true life in death, from both Mary and from God, first subject to suffering and then beyond it." Ignatius offers a series of apparent contradictions. We might ask, *How can someone be both born and unborn? How can a person find true life in death?* Ignatius lists a series of apparent contradictions that are only compatible in Jesus Christ. He presents Jesus as a mystery wherein the impossible is made possible.

Elements of this idea continue into more robust theologies in subsequent centuries. The Church will – after centuries of dispute – conclude that Jesus was both flesh and spirit, from both Mary and God. The voice of Ignatius is important in that it shows how early in the life of the Church these paradoxical ideas about Jesus appeared.

Conclusion

The first stories about Jesus – indeed those considered historical by their authors – were already theological, metaphorical, and symbolic. This is to be expected of highly significant figures. When we tell stories about figures in history, we create meaning from their impact and project our own interpretations onto their lives. We try to make sense of the lives of important people by connecting their biographies to larger cultural concerns, mythologies, and commonly held ideals.

Jesus's followers did their best to connect his words and deeds to the national symbols, prophecies, and narratives of Israel. Therefore, if you had asked a first-generation Christian why Jesus was significant, you would probably get a theological response: *Jesus is the bread of life; Jesus is the Lord's anointed one; Jesus is the mouthpiece of God on earth; Jesus is risen and vindicated.*

As a matter of course, a variety of theological teachings emerged about Jesus. Different storytellers made sense of Jesus in different ways. In the first two centuries of Christianity, as house churches saw the need for an official and uniformed theology, certain narratives emerged as authoritative. In retrospect, how-ever, we must appreciate the various ways that Jesus took storied shape. Each ancient text represents an important story in its own right. I would argue that we must resist the temptation to force the various first-century stories about Jesus into a single narrative. On the other hand, each story derives in some way from Jesus's historical impact.

Five books about Jesus in early Christian literature

Burridge, R.A. *What Are the Gospels? A Comparison with Graeco-Roman Biography*. (2nd edn; The Biblical Resource Series; Grand Rapids: Eerdmans, 2004).

Green, J.B. *The Theology of the Gospel of Luke*. (New Testament Theology; Cambridge: Cambridge University Press, 1995).

Hooker, M.D. *Not Ashamed of the Gospel: New Testament Interpretations of the Death of Christ*. (Eugene: Wipf and Stock Publishers, 2004).

Reinhartz, A. *Befriending The Beloved Disciple: A Jewish Reading of the Gospel of John*. (London: Bloomsbury Academic, 2002).

Snodgrass, K.R. *Stories with Intent: A Comprehensive Guide to the Parables of Jesus* (Grand Rapids: Eerdmans, 2008).

3

Jesus in the premodern imagination

"Place your mind before the mirror of eternity."

Saint Clare of Assisi

Introduction: Ten-thousand faces

From the second-century forward, the literature, visual depictions, and theological propositions about Jesus explode into the thousands. In many ways, the story of Jesus's changing image is the story of Christendom and Western culture more generally. The story about Jesus gives birth to Christianity, and Christianity continues to birth new Jesuses to suit its agendas.

Christianity begins in obscurity. It is only noticed by Rome when the Christians gain a reputation for refusing to worship the Roman gods.* Their numbers and geographical representation expand at a remarkable rate. After short periods of persecution, Christianity is normalized. The fourth century witnesses the worst persecution of Christians, alongside robust theological debates, and the unlikely adoption of Christianity by a Roman emperor. Whether it was religious experience, political

---

* See for example, the second-century letter by Pliny the Younger to Trajan referred to earlier.

maneuvering, or both, Constantine adopts Christianity. Within a century of the darkest days of persecution, Christianity becomes the state religion of the Empire. Christian leaders meet to formally agree on doctrine, again and again. The winners of these debates – claiming Apostolic succession and orthodoxy – will establish an infrastructure for unprecedented religious power. The losers will be labeled heretics and will be marginalized or killed. Christianity eventually forsakes all moorings to its Jewish identity. As Christianity grows, the world will become even more hostile to Jewish life. Christianity outlives the Roman Empire. The fault lines of theology and politics foreshadow massive fissures in the Church. East and West divorce in the Great Schism (1054 CE) between Eastern Orthodox and Roman Catholic churches. Massive Christian armies will be called to war against Muslims.

Institutional Christianity will produce some of the greatest art and architecture the world has ever seen. It will witness and exploit the invention of romantic love, the printing press, and global colonization. Christians will commit ten thousands calamities and inspire ten thousand felicities. And along each stage, Jesus will take on a new face to suit the times.

The cross of Jesus will comfort persecuted Christians. It will also emblazon the shields of crusading soldiers. Jesus will be painted as a modest shepherd and an enthroned king. He will be depicted in expensive, flowing robes, and all but naked on countless crucifixes. He will float above his disciples, and lie dead in Mary's arms. Some will argue that Jesus was a phantom; others, that he never had a bowel movement. In the visions of artists, Jesus will become a Constantinopolitan, a Roman, and a European. Passion plays on European stages will fan old hatreds; Christians will leave these plays to set fire to synagogues in the name of their Lord. Jesus, son of Mary, will become a prophetic forerunner to Mohammed. He will be appropriated by the ideology of asceticism and the religion of the Celts. Christ's head will be minted on gold coins. His name will be lent to cathedrals. Jesus will become a model for St Francis and St Clare, who seek lives of simplicity and pacifism. He will become a lamb and a donkey.

The key elements of this section will be expansion and evolution. It will be impossible to track any single trajectory of development. The branching effects of expansion make it difficult to chart the evolution of Jesus in all parts of emerging Christendom. That said, if we are to understand how and why Jesus took different shapes in Western commemoration, we must also sketch a few important streams of Christian history. Consider just a few key developments by comparing the end of the first century to the end of the second.

From 100 to 200 CE, Christianity evolved from a grassroots group of common folk. Some had an education but very few were wealthy enough to study theology without also having a primary method of income. By the end of the second century, defining a coherent theology became an important enterprise for many intellectual elites.

From 100 to 200 CE, the leadership of women within the Church was suppressed. The New Testament and other early sources indicate that a number of women were respected leaders in the first century. By the end of the second century, however, the bishops, elders, and deacons of the Church look to be almost exclusively male.

From 100 to 200 CE, many Christians began to imagine Jesus as an entirely heavenly being. Jesus's literal, physical body was questioned. Perhaps he was a spirit with only a veneer of a body. Jesus never left footprints, from this point of view, because his feet always hovered just above the ground. Those who maintained the belief that Jesus was indeed fully human endeavored to put down this heresy. But by the end of the second century there were camps of Christians who refused to believe that Jesus was ever fully human. Several voices in this debate meant that several different portraits of Jesus developed.

In the Christianized West, defining the significance of Jesus Christ is most commonly a process of collective self-definition. Jesus is an evolving idea that follows the changing identity of the groups who commemorate him.

Christ, not Judaism (circa second century)

From the very beginning of Christian thought, defining Jesus was a process of self-definition. The earliest house churches in the mid-first century thought of themselves as the "Body of Christ." Jesus Christ was the head of this body. Paul encourages Christians to embrace a new identity "in Christ" (this is an important phrase for him) as they commemorate Jesus's burial and resurrection. Even so, the first followers of Jesus were Jewish. They may have rethought their orientation to the Jerusalem Temple, but there is no evidence that becoming a member of the group meant giving up their Jewishness.

For these Christians, the fact that Jesus was Jewish was taken for granted. It might be debated whether Jesus was from the line of David or not, but the fact that he was a Jew was assumed. Indeed, some of the earliest non-Jewish followers attempted to show their allegiance to a Jewish messiah by external gestures of Jewishness: circumcision, diet, etc. Paul was determined that the Body of Christ should not become an exclusively Jewish club. Little did he know that a century later the problem would be reversed. By 150 CE, many Christians would openly reject any elements of Jewish thought or practice within Christianity. This development would have been unthinkable to Jesus, Mary, Peter, John, etc. While there was still Jewish and Christian cross-pollination in various communities, Christianity was becoming an exclusively non-Jewish club.

Many Christians endeavored to define themselves over and against Jewish life (what they began to call "Judaism"). To be a follower of Jesus Christ meant casting off the ways of Jewish life. In the second half of the first century, Ignatius of Antioch wrote: "If we live in accordance with Judaism, we confess that we have not received grace… It is monstrous to confess Jesus Christ and to practice Judaism" (Magnesians 8.1, 10.3).*

MEET THIS WORD: DEMIURGE

Demiurge comes from *dēmiourgos*, which was a title for public builders in the Greek-speaking world. But it also took on a theological meaning: the title was applied to a world-building deity. Lesser in rank than the supreme god, the demiurge, or "great workman," is the one who shaped and crafted the world into being. But the demiurge did not have the ability to create something from nothing; he simply crafted with pre-existing materials. Hence he is classed as a secondary world-building deity. This idea was made popular in Platonic thought and became fodder for argument in some circles of early Christianity.

By the second century, Marcion of Sinope had taken on a similar concern.** Marcion was the son of a bishop and an influential voice in Christian leadership. He sought to purify Christianity of all Jewish elements. His first step was to label the God of the Hebrew scriptures (the "Old Testament") a rigid and evil demiurge. Marcion therefore attempted to create a purified Christian Bible without the Old Testament, with ten letters of Paul, and a version of Luke's gospel. The aim was to eliminate obvious

---

* It is possible that Ignatus is referring not to "Judaism" but to Judaizing. If so, this would be a condemnation of those who encourage non-Jews to act Jewish, or do so themselves.

** Marcion's life is difficult to date, but his ideas look to have taken hold in the early second century.

appeals to Hebrew scripture that can be found in Christian writings. So Luke was redacted to eliminate any obvious quotations from Hebrew scripture. A new portrait of Jesus thus emerges.

According to Marcion, Jesus was not the Jewish messiah. Jesus was the Christ. He was God. Jesus had nothing to do with Judaism. Marcion supposed that the Jewish messiah would come later, perhaps to establish a kingdom for Israel. But Jesus was not this messiah. Such a statement would have been incomprehensible to the first generation of Jesus's followers, and many of Marcion's contemporaries refused to accept his point of view.

Other Christian leaders (including Justin Martyr, Irenaeus, Rhodon and Tertullian) exerted considerable effort to combat Marcion's agenda. They would fight for the inclusion of the Torah, Prophets and Writings. They fought for a traditional view of Jesus's lineage. But while Marcion and his followers are remembered as heretics, the damage inflicted on the Christian imagination would stick. Jesus would become less and less attached to Judaism in the minds of Christians.

The Alexamenos graffito (circa second century)

One of the earliest – perhaps *the* earliest – surviving portraits of Jesus depicts him with the head of a donkey. We call it the "Alexamenos graffito" because it was etched as graffiti meant to ridicule a Christian named Alexamenos.

This etching features two figures: a man below, and a man above (with a donkey's head) on a T-shaped cross. The Greek writing can be roughly translated: "Alexamenos worships his god." It does not use the name Jesus, but the etching does show a "god" hanging from the cross. When this was etched (around the second century), Jesus is the only known figure that was both crucified and worshipped as a god. This artifact reminds us what

Figure 12 Alexamenos graffito, circa 200 CE.

an odd and unique combination this was! Whoever Alexamenos was – and we only know what is suggested by the graffito – he seems to have been the source of ironic humor: crucifixion ought to be altogether shaming but Alexamenos seems to honor a crucified figure as if he is worshipping a god.

The fact that this god is pictured with a donkey's head suggests great dishonor, and underscores the absurdity of this act of worship. Or perhaps the donkey's head echoes rumors that Jews and Christians worshipped the image of a donkey. (Tertullian, a Christian scholar writing in the late second and early third centuries, acknowledges that this rumor exists.) In either case, the image of a crucified god with the head of a donkey was unflattering in the extreme. Those who embraced Jesus after his death embraced something that Paul rightly calls "foolishness to the Greeks" in his first letter to Corinth. From their humble beginnings to their popularity in later centuries, Christians had to contend with the shame associated with the cross. This might explain why the symbol of the cross becomes a source of pride. Perhaps Christians like Alexamenos, who were mocked because of their association with Jesus, wore this shame like a badge of honor to defend against public ridicule.

This etching also confirms that commemorations of Jesus tend toward the symbolic. As a historical figure, Jesus is a man who looks like other first-century men in the Mediterranean but he is packaged in symbolic imagery in public memory. Because of his legacy, he becomes a symbol of resurrection and divinity for Christians, and a symbol of foolishness for others.

Valentinus and the sexualized Jesus (circa second and third centuries)

Valentinus (circa 100–160 CE) – perhaps a student of Theudas, a student of Paul – has been labeled "gnostic" in Christian history. Thus Valentinus represents Christian heresy in retrospect. His school of thought extended well into the fourth century, branching both East and West.* Valentinus, it seems, was almost entirely

---

* In this context, "East and West" refers to the emerging geographical hubs of Christianity in (what is now considered) Turkey and Italy.

disinterested or unaware of Jesus's life as a historical figure. Jesus becomes an almost entirely spiritual figure in Valentinian thought. For example, Valentinus is purported to have said: "Jesus digested divinity; he ate and drank in a special way, without excreting his solids. He had such a great capacity for continence that the nourishment within him was not corrupted, for he did not experience corruption."* Whether Valentinus actually said this is less important than what is revealed about how Jesus's legacy was evolving in the second century. Jesus's humanity was diminished so that his divinity could be exalted. This represents a shift away from Paul's thought: Paul believed that Jesus's humanity was integral to his personhood. Paul (and John) emphasized Jesus's birth "according to the flesh" but, by the time of Valentinus, some believed that Jesus was so spiritual that he never had a bowel movement.

One of the writings that emerged from this school was the Gospel of Philip (composed between 180–250 CE). Philip transforms Jesus into a representative of a cryptic and symbolic system of thought. Christians following Valentinus used insider language meant to seem mysterious to outsiders. Indeed, this text talks more about Jesus in terms of spiritual and heavenly symbolism than it does about Jesus's life on earth. This is also a text that spiritualizes sexuality and suggests that Jesus and Mary Magdalene were intimate.

MEET THIS WORD: LACUNA

Lacuna refers to a gap or a missing part. When it is used in the study of ancient texts, a lacuna is a missing letter, word, or group of words in a document. The plural of lacuna is lacunae. A lacuna may be caused by erosion, worms, mice, mishandling, etc. For example, in the Gospel of Philip, verse 59, is fragmentary: "and...companion

---

* Quoted by Clement of Alexandria, *Stromateis*, 3.59.3; cf. also *Miscellanies*, 3.7.

MEET THIS WORD: LACUNA (*cont.*)

of the...Mary Magdalene...used to...more than the disciples...kiss her...times the rest." These lacunae in the text offer a challenge to modern translators: not only must we decipher the best English translations from the original Coptic, we must supply the missing words. Most translations render verse 59 like this: "Jesus loved her more than all the disciples, and used to kiss her often on her mouth."

The Gospel of Philip tells us that Mary Magdalene was the "lover" of Jesus. Although this verse contains several lacunae and is therefore difficult to translate, it suggests that he "loved her more than all the disciples, and used to kiss her often on her mouth" (59). Of course, this detail allows the author to extend the jealousy theme. The male disciples ask: "Why do you love her more than all of us?"* The trouble with reading this in a literal sexual way is that the Gospel of Philip is not a literal-sense sort of document. In fact, one of the unique features is its elitism: only elite members of their in-group were able to understand the hidden meaning of the words used.

The school of thought that produced this gospel believed that words were unable to capture reality. The words "mother, sister, and lover" (36) were symbols that transcended common meaning. If we were to take these words literally, this author would probably accuse us of being "unworthy of life" because "the words we give to earthly realities engender illusion" (11). You really don't get more elitist than this. Bart Ehrman explains that books such as the Gospel of Philip "are for insiders who – unlike us – already

---

* Some argue that "kiss her often on the feet" is a better translation. In fact, this gospel is fragmentary and so reconstructing this line is very difficult. My thanks to Mark Goodacre for this insight.

have all the background information they need."* Really, nothing in this gospel is intended to be taken at face value.

Because of the Valentinians' fondness for symbol, mystery, and metaphor, it is difficult to tell how much of their sex talk represents practice. Many scholars think that the Valentinians were all talk – that they used sexual metaphor to describe their spiritual ecstasy. Others believe that spiritual ecstasy was achieved through physical enactment. In either case, Valentinian writings reveal much more about their unique philosophy and very little about Jesus's sexuality.

With this in mind, here is a possible reconstruction of Valentinian theology. In order to describe how a singular God could create such a diverse world, the Valentinians imagined that God the Father projected his thought, and that this thought took the form of "Intellect" (male) and "Truth" (female). In this theology, Intellect and Truth are not just attributes of God; they become distinct personalities. Intellect and Truth then produced another pair of male and female counterparts, and that pair produced another, and so on. Each pair was one step removed from God the Father, but all of these existed within the mind of God. Importantly, each pair was a masculine and feminine union. But one of the lowest projections was a feminine form called "Wisdom." She divorced herself from her male counterpart and attempted to gain direct knowledge of God. This ruined the harmonious balance of the cosmos, and it was this misinformed personality that created the material world. The Gospel of Philip says that: "The world came into being through an error" (99). The Valentinians believed that physical gender is not indicative of the collective gender of the human race. They believed that all human spirits are female. Humanity therefore represents female

---

* Ehrman, B.D., *Lost Christianities: The Battles for Scripture and the Faiths We Never Knew* (New York: Oxford University Press, 2005), p. 122.

elements that derive from masculine (angelic) counterparts. In this view, humans will continue to be alienated from the mind of God until they are united with their higher, masculine selves at the end of time.

For the Valentinians, spiritual marriage between male and female was a way to correct the corruption of the material world. Jesus's spiritual union with his ideal disciple is a key symbol along these lines. Jesus, therefore, becomes a way to transcend the physical world and become whole.

Jesus and a woman accused of adultery (circa third century)

Open any Bible with a New Testament and flip to John 8. There you'll find a story about a woman accused of adultery. It is now a very popular story about Jesus's interaction with men who wish to execute her, Jesus's clever admonition to avoid judgment, and his word of advice to the woman he has saved from death. But this story was not always part of the Gospel of John, and is in fact absent from the earliest manuscripts. Indeed, it seems to have been added to the gospel around the third century CE.* (In later centuries the story was inserted into Luke's gospel.) John 8 begins:

> Early in the morning [Jesus] came again to the temple. All the people came to him and he sat down and began to teach them. The scribes and the Pharisees brought a woman who had been caught in adultery; and making her stand before all of them, they said to him, "Teacher, this woman was caught in the very act of committing adultery. Now

---

* For a book-length account of this story, see Keith, C., *The Pericope Adulterae, The Gospel of John, and the Literacy of Jesus*. New Testament Tools, Studies, and Documents 38 (Leiden: Brill, 2009).

in the law Moses commanded us to stone such women. Now what do you say?" They said this to test him, so that they might have some charge to bring against him. Jesus bent down and wrote with his finger on the ground. When they kept on questioning him, he straightened up and said to them, "Let anyone among you who is without sin be the first to throw a stone at her." And once again he bent down and wrote on the ground. When they heard it, they went away, one by one, beginning with the elders; and Jesus was left alone with the woman standing before him. Jesus straightened up and said to her, "Woman, where are they? Has no one condemned you?" She said, "No one, sir." And Jesus said, "Neither do I condemn you. Go your way, and from now on do not sin again."

The story of the nameless woman accused of adultery probably does not reflect a historical event in the life of Jesus. Even so, it preserves an important lesson about caution when punishing others for their perceived sins. In this way, it might reflect an important truth about Jesus's character and his ethics. But it also reflects what some second- and third-century Christians thought about Jesus.

Similar to other stories about Jesus in the gospels, a dilemma is posed to Jesus by other Jewish leaders. Will Jesus prove himself faithful to the teaching of Moses about adultery? Or will he prove himself compassionate (also an important Jewish ideal)? It is also possible that summary executions of this kind were forbidden by Roman law (i.e. Rome prohibited Jews from enacting capital punishment). So Jesus encounters a complex puzzle of social expectations and legal realities in this story.

Jesus delays his answer by writing on the ground with his finger. He then answers (as he does elsewhere in the gospels) with a single, pithy reply. In this case, he says, "Let anyone among you who is without sin be the first to throw a stone at her." Jesus says no more, but continues to write on the ground. The fact that none of the woman's accusers assault her suggests that they were (1) self-aware of their own sin, and (2) agreed with Jesus's logic.

After a brief exchange with the woman, Jesus advises her not to sin again, and refuses to condemn her.

Although this story was only later inserted into John's gospel, it seems to fit well with Jesus's character and ethics as portrayed in first-century documents. There is one characteristic, however, that is unique to this story. Nowhere else in the gospels do we see Jesus's ability to write. Indeed, Jesus is most commonly perceived to be a member of the manual labor caste in a society that was largely illiterate. That Jesus is portrayed as being able to write is therefore remarkable. Chris Keith – an expert on ancient literacy – explains:

> Most likely, John 8:6, John 8:8 represents simply a claim that Jesus could write – a claim quite significant in the ancient world, where most individuals were illiterate. Such a claim also explains why a scribe inserted the passage after John 7, where the Jewish leaders question both Jesus's literacy specifically (John 7:15) and Galileans' knowledge of the law and ability to search it generally (John 7:49, John 7:52)*

Could it be that Jesus's social status as a manual laborer continued to be a source of discomfort for some second- and third-century Christians? Think of it this way: Christianity evolved from a grassroots movement among people of low social status to a sophisticated theology shaped by highly educated elites. Perhaps, as the social standing of Christians evolved, their questions (and answers) about Jesus evolved accordingly. In this case, we see Jesus portrayed as a highly educated interpreter of Moses's law able to supersede even the elders among the scribes and Pharisees.

---

* Keith, C., *Manuscript History and John 8:1–11*. [Online]. (URL http://www.bibleodyssey.org/passages/related-articles/Manuscript%20 History%20and%20John.aspx). Society of Biblical Literature (Accessed March 29, 2018).

First Council of Nicaea (fourth century)

By the fourth century, Christianity had become a social force within the Roman Empire. Many urban centers hosted house churches (overseers or bishops assumed geographical leadership). Due to the ever-increasing number of Christians, it was impossible for all the Christians within a city to worship in the same house church. These small rooms simply could not hold all the Christian residents of the city. Various house churches attempted to demonstrate solidarity by sharing the same bread for communion and praying for the leaders of other churches. But the theme of unity – that was so very important to Paul – was difficult to achieve, even within a single city. Communities were invariably divided by geography, social status, wealth, and ideology. Any semblance of a common belief system became extremely difficult to maintain. For example, followers for the most part would confess the "Lordship" of Christ, but different Christians had different ideas about what was meant by the term "Lord."

In the early fourth century, the Roman Emperor Diocletian was convinced that Christianity was a threat to Empire in both ideology and practice. He banned Christians from gathering for worship. Churches were burned, as were their holy texts. Diocletian publicly executed prominent Christians. This period marked the most intense form of persecution that Christianity had yet seen. Many churches were forced to disband, relocate, or meet in secret, which further exacerbated the problem of open communication and common understanding among church leaders. For a system of belief that required a common understanding of Jesus Christ – his identity, nature, and significance – persecution posed another enormous obstacle.

Enter Constantine (circa 272–337 CE). After a complicated retirement by Diocletian and an even more complicated rise to power by Constantine, Christianity became a legal religion within the Empire (313 CE).* Constantine wanted peace within the Empire and hoped to achieve it through a unity of religious practice. He adopted Christianity as his own religion, and created the first ecumenical Council of Christian leaders in Nicaea in 325 CE in Asia Minor (modern-day Turkey).

One of the most important topics discussed at this Council was the nature of Christ. Two of the most important voices in this debate were Alexander and Arius (both leaders in Alexandria, Egypt). Eusebius of Nicomedia spoke for the Arian camp at the Council, but the debate predated the official meeting in Nicaea.

Borrowing from the Gospel of John, and the writings of Justin Martyr and Origen, the voices in that conversation used the term "Logos" to refer to Jesus as a divine being. The first lines of the Gospel of John read:

> In the beginning was the Word (*Logos*), and the Word was with God, and the Word was God. He was in the beginning with God. All things came into being through him, and without him not one thing came into being.

In this context, the Greek word *Logos* represents Jesus as he existed as God created the world. Both the camps agreed that Christ existed alongside God during the creation of the world. Allow me to emphasize: *both sides of the debate agreed that Jesus existed before he was born.*

The key point of dispute concerned the question of "coequality": *Was the Logos equal with God?* Put another way: *Did Jesus Christ exist before creation?* Alexander's camp answered yes. The Arians answered no. According to the Arian view, Christ was the

---

* A fuller treatment of this period would detail severe economic troubles and the slow demise of the Republic. Diocletian attempted to institute a new system of government – the Tetrarchy – whereby the wider Empire was ruled by four emperors. When Constantine rose to power, he ruled Britain, Gaul, and Spain.

Figure 13 Alpha and omega: This fourth-century mural from the catacomb of Commodilla depicts Jesus between the first and last letters of the Greek alphabet, suggesting that Jesus was actually present when time began and moreover will be present when it concludes. The artist thus reflects the Christian doctrine that Jesus exists alongside God, the Creator.

first created being. This – now called the Arian controversy – provoked riots in the streets of Alexandria.

Constantine, by convening the Council, could not have anticipated the heat of this debate. Leaders from all over the Empire attended. Most did not have a strong opinion about the debate. It soon became clear, however, that Alexander's camp was livid over the matter. The anti-Arians were prepared to divide the Church. Recognizing the stakes, the majority decided to draw up a creed that would exclude the Arian camp. The result is what we now call the Nicene Creed:

> We believe in one God, the Father Almighty, maker of all things visible and invisible. And in one Lord Jesus Christ, the Son of God, the only-begotten of the Father; that is, of the essence of the Father, God of God, Light of Light, very God of very God, begotten, not made, being of one substance with the Father; by whom all things were made both in heaven and on earth; who for us men, and for our salvation, came down and was incarnate and was made man; he suffered, and the third day he rose again, ascended into heaven; from thence he shall come to judge the quick and the dead.
>
> And in the Holy Ghost.
>
> But those who say: "There was a time when he was not," and "He was not before he was made," and "He was made out of nothing," or "He is of another substance" or "essence," or "The Son of God is created," or "changeable," or "alterable" – they are condemned by the holy catholic and apostolic Church.

Arius lost the debate and died in exile (although his camp would continue to exert influence). Constantine's Church decided that Father and Son were equal. This was a victory for those defending the Trinitarian slogan: "three persons, one substance." The Son of God would not be viewed as a subordinate member of the Trinity in official doctrine. Jesus was officially an eternal being, having no beginning and no end.

Jesus, the Good Shepherd (circa fourth century)

In some of the earliest visual images of Jesus, he is portrayed as a "Good Shepherd." These paintings and statues often depict him carrying a lamb on his shoulders while securing the animal's hoofs with his hands. The theme echoes John 10 most directly, wherein Jesus calls himself the Good Shepherd. Shepherding is mentioned several times in the New Testament. Numerous passages in the Hebrew Bible also associate the king of Israel with shepherding.

But centuries before Jesus walked the earth, Greek and Roman sculptors popularized this image. Not surprisingly, Christian artists were influenced by the artistic expressions of their cultures. It could be that the Greek myth of the *Kriophoros* (a boy carrying a ram who saved his city) was influential here, or the Roman image of the *Moschophoros* (a boy carrying a calf, modeling a faithful worshipper). For Christian artists, Jesus takes on a similar theme.

One possible explanation for its popularity among Christians relates to their fear of persecution. A more obvious portrait of Jesus might invite defacement or destruction. But because images were common of boys holding animals, this commemoration of Jesus could hide in plain sight. Whatever the case, the popularity of Jesus as Shepherd continued beyond the era of persecution. The following mosaic draws from the same theme well after Christianity was adopted as the state religion in 380 CE.*

This image of Jesus remains ubiquitous in popular Christian art today. It is worth pointing out, however, that nowhere in the Bible does Jesus actually pick up and carry a lamb.

---

* Christianity was made legal by Constantine several decades earlier, but it did not become the state religion until the late fourth century.

Figure 14 Moschophoros sculpture (circa 570 BCE): This sculpture of a man shouldering a calf was excavated at the Acropolis, Athens.

Figure 15 Mural of the Good Shepherd: This mural of Christ in the Catacomb of Priscilla in Rome might date as early as the third century. Notice that Jesus is beardless and without flowing robes (made iconic in later art). The shepherding theme is one of the earliest and most popular images for Jesus in Christian art.

Figure 16 Mosaic of Jesus the Good Shepherd (circa 450 CE) in the interior of the Mausoleum of Galla Placidia: She ruled as queen regent (on behalf of her son), and in doing so fulfilled all the duties of a Roman Emperor from 423–37 CE. Jesus is here depicted with Roman features and clothing that bespeaks great wealth, while retaining the humble occupation of a shepherd. The golden aureole around his head reinforces his heavenly status.

Augustine on the Trinity (fifth century)

Augustine of Hippo (circa 354–430 CE) was a North African theologian and bishop. It would be difficult to overstate his impact on Western religion and philosophy. His writings cover topics related to cosmology, epistemology, politics, ethics, and anthropology (just to name a few). But he is most celebrated for his impact on Christian theology.

One of the most important words in the Christian vocabulary is "Trinity." Christians believe (almost universally) that Jesus is both the "Son of God" and God. As God, Jesus is intimately and integrally related to God as "Father" and God as "Spirit." Jesus is often called the "Son," the "Logos," or the "Second Person" of the Trinity. In this way, God is said to be triune (*tri* = three; *unus* = one). But the word Trinity is not used in the Bible.

Ignatius of Antioch, Justin Martyr, Tertullian of Carthage, and other early Christian scholars make explicit affirmations of the triune nature of God. Tertullian, for example, reads John's gospel through a Trinitarian lens: Jesus says, "The Father and I are one" (John 10:30). Tertullian, referring to Father, Son, and Paraclete (Holy Spirit), writes that "these three are one substance, not one person, in the sense in which it was said, 'I and the Father are one' in respect of unity of substance, not of singularity of number" (*Against Praxeas* 25). It was not uncommon for early Christian interpreters of the Bible to assume God's triune nature, even if the text itself did not make this doctrine explicit. Several passages within the New Testament do suggest that the metaphors of Father, Son, and Spirit can be applied to God. But the idea was still germinating when the authors of the New Testament were writing. Arguably, the doctrine did not fully flower until Gregory of Nazianzus in the fourth century and Augustine of Hippo in the early fifth century.

MEET THIS WORD: BAPTISM

Baptism comes from the Greek word *baptismos*, which denotes immersion or ritual washing. Early Christianity adapted this Jewish ritual for purification and turned it into an initiation rite. In Christian practice, baptism is the ritual practice involving water (either by administering water to the head or by full-body immersion), whereby new members become one with Christ and one with the Church. The key symbolic value of baptism is its resemblance to burial and resurrection. To show solidarity with Jesus, who was buried and raised from dead, Christians participate in a symbolic dying and rising. In Catholic doctrine, it is called the "first sacrament" and the doorway into the Christian faith. Many denominations within Christianity use baptism as a metaphor for spiritual awakening whereby the Holy Spirit of God is experienced more fully.

Augustine's fifteen-part treatise, called *On the Trinity*, attempts to explain the triune nature of God: *How is it that many (three) can be of one substance?* And of equal importance to Augustine: *How does humanity participate in the oneness of God?* In order to explain this, Jesus's person and a selection of his teachings provide a model.

Humanity, according to Augustine, is prone to discord because of sin. God, on the other hand, might be thought of as the ultimate harmony. He writes: "By wickedness and ungodliness with a crashing discord we had bounced away, and flowed and faded away from the one supreme true God into the many, divided by the many, clinging to the many." Not only is humanity out of tune with God, it is out of tune with itself. But through Christ, argues Augustine, the discordant many become one. Christ, being one with God, also draws humanity to this unity. As believers enact Jesus's death and resurrection in baptism they rise "with him in spirit through faith." This allows humanity to be drawn together and drawn to God so that "we may be able to cling to the one, enjoy the one, and remain for ever one" (*On the Trinity* 4.11).*

Augustine appeals again to Jesus's claim that "The Father and I are one" (John 10:30). He also appeals to John 17:20–2, where Jesus prays: "I ask not only on behalf of these, but also on behalf of those who will believe in me through their word, that they may all be one. As you, Father, are in me and I am in you, may they also be in us." For Augustine, harmony within humanity is possible because God (the many that are one) makes it possible (*On the Trinity* 4.12). Such is the nature of a generous and compassionate God.

In part fifteen, Augustine writes:

---

* Translation from Edmund Hill in Saint Augustine, *The Trinity (de Trinitate)*. (Hyde Park, New York: New City Press, 1991).

We have talked enough about the Father and the Son insofar as we have been able to see them through this mirror and in this puzzle. Now we must discuss the Holy Spirit as far as it is granted us with God's help to see him. According to the holy scriptures this Holy Spirit is not just the Father's alone nor the Son's alone, but the Spirit of them both, and thus he suggests to us the common charity [or gift] by which the Father and the Son love each other. (*On the Trinity* 15.27)

In a sense, the Trinity is a model for loving relationships. In explaining the Trinity, Augustine is teaching the Church how to relate to God. This assumes that God is fundamentally relational and humanity is too.

The Gospel of Gamaliel (circa fifth century)

Ever since Mark's first gospel in the first century CE, stories about Jesus (or loosely related to Christian belief) circulated under the genre of "gospel." Many of these so-called gospels purport to be from eyewitnesses of Jesus's life. One such story, which emerged in the fifth or sixth century, purported to be from Rabbi Gamaliel's perspective. Scholars now call this the Gospel of Gamaliel, but it is never referred to by this title in ancient literature. It survives in several languages, including Arabic and Ethiopic. The fullest version of this short account is included in Ethiopic (within a text titled *Lament of the Virgin*), but it looks to have been originally written in Coptic. The central message of this story is that Jesus was indeed resurrected, despite the efforts of "the Jews" to produce a false body and thus deceive Pilate. In short, this is revisionist history using a pseudonym for the purpose of promoting Christian doctrine and anti-Jewish dogma.

The narrator claims to be an eyewitness and speaks in the first person: "I, Gamaliel, walked with the crowds and witnessed all what happened in the tomb of my Lord Jesus, and the great fight that Pilate undertook against the High Priests."* Thus the author uses the name of the first-century rabbi mentioned in Acts 5:34 and 22:3, and in *Rosh Hashanah* 2:8–9 of the Mishnah (some Jewish traditions refer to him as "Gamaliel the Elder"). But in the Gospel of Gamaliel he purportedly calls Jesus "my Lord." Moreover, he stands against the other Jewish leaders who seek to discredit Jesus's resurrection. In this way, Gamaliel becomes a voice for Christian doctrine.

Pontius Pilate, the Roman prefect over Judea, who ordered Jesus's crucifixion, becomes a key character in this text. Pilate is also portrayed as confessing Christian doctrine. The "great fight that Pilate undertook" in this gospel is that he questioned the centurions who claimed Jesus's body was stolen. Finding their testimony inconsistent, Pilate goes himself to Jesus's tomb. He discovers that "the Jews" have taken the grave-clothes (or shroud) of Jesus and placed them on the corpse of a robber who was crucified next to Jesus. Jesus's body was therefore not in the tomb, according to this gospel.

Pilate then recalls a saying of Jesus which is not found in the four canonical gospels.** According to the Gospel of Gamaliel, Jesus claimed that "dead men will rise from [my] tomb." Pilate believes this and recites this prayer over Jesus's tomb:

> I implore you today, O Lord Jesus. You are the resurrection and the life, the giver of life to all and to the dead. I believe that you rose

---

* All quotations of this text are adapted from Mingana, A. (trans.), "Lament of the Virgin" and "Martyrdom of Pilate," *Woodbrooke Studies*, 2, 1928.

** Scholars refer to sayings like this as "agrapha," which means "not written."

Figure 17 *What is Truth?* (1890, oil on canvas) by Russian realist painter, Nikolai Ge: This is Pilate's famous question to Jesus in John 18:38. Ge once said that the purpose of the artist was "to find one's thought, one's feeling in the eternal; the true is indeed the task of art." Given the artist's use of light – placing an illuminated Pilate in dramatic contrast to a darkened Jesus – it is possible that Ge saw Pilate as a model for truth seeking.

again as you appeared to me. Do not judge me, O my Lord, because I am doing this. I have not done it from fear of the Jews, nor to test your resurrection. O my Lord, I have confidence in your words and in the miracles which you have wrought. You are living because you raised many dead men. Now, O my Lord, do not be angry with me because I placed a foreign corpse in the place in which lay your body. I did this to put to shame and confusion those who deny your resurrection. To them belong shame and confusion forever and ever, and to you are due glory and honor from the mouth of your servant Pilate forever and forever and ever.

In this historical fiction, Pilate effectively reveals what Orthodox Christians in the fifth century believed about Jesus's resurrection. And it does not differ much from what might be expected from a first-century Christian. The key difference here is that it is now found on the lips of a Roman prefect. One wonders if this "conversion" of Pilate is an anachronism due to the newly found marriage of Roman government and Christian faith. The post-Constantine Christianity that produced this revisionist history was, after all, not an enemy of the Roman Empire. As such, Pilate is exonerated for his part in Jesus's execution, but the Jews continue to be demonized.

After Pilate prays over Jesus's tomb, another miracle happens. The corpse used in the plot to cover up the resurrection – the robber's body wrapped in Jesus's grave-clothes – returns to life.

And Pilate shouted with jubilation on account of the joy and happiness which filled his heart and his soul, to such an extent that the rocks echoed his voice. And he then ordered the people that were standing to lift the stone from the door of the tomb, and immediately the dead man came out walking, and he bowed before Pilate, the Governor. As to the Jews who were present, they were seized with panic, shame, and confusion, and ran away wailing secretly from their fear of the Governor.

Pilate orders his soldiers to cut down the Jews with swords. After this violence (echoing and foreshadowing a long history of Christian violence against Jews), Pilate speaks to the resurrected robber. The man relays to Pilate another saying from Jesus: "Tell my beloved Pilate to fight for my resurrection because I have decided to appoint him his portion in Paradise."

This portrait of Pilate is especially interesting because of the prominent role that he plays in the Apostles' Creed (which some date as early as the fifth century in its full form). The Apostles' Creed famously declares that Jesus "suffered under Pontius Pilate." Could it be that such a statement motivated some Christians to fictionalize Pilate's ultimate reconciliation to Jesus? Whatever the case, the Gospel of Gamaliel offers a Roman-friendly and Orthodox-friendly revision of the passion narrative. In so doing, we also see Roman-Christian hatred of Jews grow.* Finally, this text shows no evidence of existence in the first four (perhaps five) centuries of Christianity. It clearly reflects the political agendas of a post-Constantine religion.

Yeshu in the Talmud (circa fifth century)

The Talmud is one among several collections of rabbinic thought. In general, the medieval Jewish rabbis discussed various aspects of Jewish life, commented on legal instruction, interpreted ancient stories, and debated on all of the above. There are two major compositions of the Talmud – that of Jerusalem and Babylon – that collect centuries of intra-Jewish conversation and interpretation. It is important to keep in mind that trying to find any reference to Jesus in Jewish literature is like trying to find a needle in a

---

* Later in the text, Pilate is persecuted and martyred by "the Jews"; but he remains faithful to his conversion, and hopes to meet Jesus in Paradise.

haystack. By and large, these rabbis avoided the topic. That said, we do find a few mentions to a "Yeshu" (the Hebrew name for Jesus). Of course, this name would have been as common as the name Joshua. But given the prevalence of Christian persecution of Jews during this period, these texts may represent a backlash.

MEET THIS WORD: MEDIEVAL

Medieval is from the Latin word *medius*, meaning "middle." The English use of this word is modern, emerging in the first half of the 1800s. The phrase "medieval period" is used synonymously with "Middle Ages." The general framework for this period is between the demise of the Roman Empire in 476 CE and the European Renaissance in the 1300s CE. This temporal designation refers specifically to European history. Not only is this word Eurocentric, it is also Christocentric as the period in question is only seen as the "middle" if one presupposes that Jesus was the beginning of a new epoch. From the perspective of a Christian European in the 1800s, the fifth to fourteen centuries seem to represent the middle of the epoch.

If indeed the rabbis do refer to Jesus, it takes the form of vilification. In contrast to the lofty and worshipful claims of Christianity, "Yeshu" was either a fool or a false teacher. He studied magic in Egypt. Yeshu was deceptive: "Yeshu practiced magic and deceived and led Israel astray" (b. Sanh. 107b). Another text indicates that because of his false teaching, Yeshu "is going to be stoned [executed] for practicing magic and leading Israel astray" (b. Sanh. 43a). It is possible that "leading Israel astray" may refer to Christian doctrines deemed by the rabbis to promote apostasy (the state of being cast out of the religious community). The label "magician" would have been used as an insult. Magic usually referred to strange feats performed by a foreigner using unknown or demonic powers. Adding to this mythology, Yeshu embedded (tattooed?) what he learned in Egypt into his flesh.

But it is difficult to pull together a coherent portrait of Jesus from Jewish literature. Different statements from various rabbis spanning generations give us only a few vague insults. When set together, we have little more than a handful of puzzle pieces. Rabbi Michael Cook, Professor at Hebrew Union College, explains that, "some passages that were not originally about Jesus became misconstrued as such… Above all, the Jesus to whom the rabbis reacted was not the historical man but the gospels' reconfiguration of him."* The Talmud also creates confusion about Jesus's mother, accepted in Christian doctrine to be Mary. But was Jesus actually the son of Pandera or Stada? These characters are unknown in Christian history. Mary's identity is also confused. Was Mary's real name Stada? Or was she Mary Magdalene? Peter Schäfer rightly concludes that despite this name confusion, the varying Talmudic texts purport that Yeshu's mother had both a husband and a lover.**

For the sake of argument, let's momentarily assume that these rabbis intend to set the record straight concerning Jesus: *What would these claims about Yeshu reveal about Jesus?* First, the claim about Jesus's time in Egypt may come from the Gospel of Matthew. Matt. 2:13–23 claims that Jesus's family fled to Egypt to escape Herod's murderous intentions. Moreover, Matthew does not tell us how long the family remained in Egypt as refugees. Second, the claim about practicing foreign magic may derive from Jesus's accusers in Matt. 12:27. They accuse Jesus of casting out demons using the power of Beelzebul (a Canaanite deity). Third, the claim that Jesus was illegitimately born may derive from Matthew's claim that Mary was impregnated by divine

---

* Cook, M.J., *Modern Jews Engage the New Testament: Enhancing Jewish Well-Being in a Christian Environment* (Woodstock: Jewish Lights, 2008), p. 15.

** Schäfer, P., *Jesus in the Talmud* (Princeton: Princeton University Press, 2007), pp. 15–19.

means. These rabbis may well have rejected such a notion and offered a more plausible solution to Yeshu's odd birth. It is therefore possible that these Talmudic texts are designed to refute claims made by Matthew's gospel.

Jesus's illustrated life (circa fifth century)

In the early Christian art surveyed in this chapter, Jesus takes symbolic shape. Rather than depicting the man, Jesus is indicated by metaphor (e.g. a shepherd boy). As Christianity expands and grows wealthy, more explicit and biographical portraits emerge. Scenes from biblical stories become subjects for art. This development will occupy centuries of artistic expression and carry some of history's great masters to prominence.

One of the earliest examples of biographical illustration of Jesus's life is this fifth-century Byzantine panel in ivory. It shows three scenes from the gospels: Herod's murder of infants (Matt. 2); the baptism of Jesus by John the Baptist (Matt. 3 and parallels); and Jesus's transformation of water into wine (John 2).

Notice that the artist is not reading from a single gospel narrative. Herod's murder of infants is only found in Matthew; Jesus's provision of wine at Cana is only found in John. This suggests that the various accounts of Jesus's life have been merged in the artist's mind (or the mind of the person who commissioned this piece). The artist, however, may not have a strong grasp of the gospel narratives, given that Jesus is shown as a child during his baptism.

Another development mirrored in this panel is that Jesus is wearing his iconic robes. In the first scene, the murderous Roman soldier is wearing a common tunic. The tunic is short, leaving his knees exposed. So too, John the Baptist's garb fails to cover his legs. This would have been common dress in the first century, and

Figure 18 Panel in ivory (circa fifth century CE).

Jesus probably wore a simple tunic too. Flowing robes were the garb of the wealthy; notice Herod's attire in the first scene. But in the last water-into-wine scene, Jesus is wearing flowing robes, usually reserved for the wealthy. Jesus has also received his haloed aureole in the second two scenes.

The move to visually represent scenes from the gospels became a trend and was eventually made official doctrine. In

629 CE, the Council of Constantinople declared that, "instead of the lamb, our Lord Jesus Christ will be shown hereafter in his human form in images so that we shall be led to remember his mortal life, his passion, and his death, which paid the ransom for mankind."

Christmas time (sixth century)

In the first six centuries of Christian expansion, Christianity was practiced somewhat differently from city to city (and importantly, from East to West). The date established for Jesus's birth is an example of this variety. By the end of the second century, May 20, March 21, and multiple dates in April were suggested for Jesus's birthdate (I specify these dates using the modern calendar for clarity). Some Eastern cities celebrated Jesus's birth on what we now consider to be January 6. Concurrently, many other cities celebrated Jesus's birth on what we now consider December 25. But it wasn't until the sixth century that December 25 became the standard date for most cities.

While the subject of Jesus's birth was interesting to Christians as early as the first century, our earliest sources – Paul's letters and Mark's gospel – do not include a nativity story. And while Paul mentions a commemorative festival related to Jesus's death (1 Cor. 5:7–8), there is no evidence that the nativity stories of Matthew and Luke were celebrated as annual feasts until centuries later. And because neither Matthew nor Luke suggest a date for Jesus's birth, later theologians were left to suggest, guess, and surmise when Jesus might have been born. December 25 was probably not seriously considered until the fourth century.

While Jesus's birthdate was unknown to his first-century followers and disputed among later theologians, one assumption was common: every writer on this topic believed that Jesus's birth was a theological event. In other words, God got involved and so the date probably wasn't random. Whatever date it was, it would have to be theologically significant. Using this premise, it became commonplace to believe that Jesus was crucified on the same date that he was divinely conceived. Surmising that Jesus was crucified on March 25 (John's gospel associates Jesus's crucifixion with the Jewish Passover feast), some theologians guessed that Jesus was also conceived on March 25. While the logic that connected theological dates might seem odd to modern folk, it would have seemed natural to ancient and medieval minds. The thought was that significant events were never random. God's plan of salvation had been carefully bound together, so patterns were to be expected.

Because many Christians believed that Jesus was conceived on March 25, they looked to December 25 as a logical birthdate, as it is nine months after conception. Others believed that Jesus was both crucified and conceived on April 6. Thus January 6 (being nine months later than April 6) made better sense. In keeping with the logic that great theological events happen on important theological dates, many Christians also believed that Jesus's baptism also happened on January 6.*

The difference between December 25 and January 6 explains two things: first, why some churches eventually held feasts on both dates; second, the tradition that there are twelve days of Christmas (the time between December 25 and January 6). The logic used to determine these dates is certainly intriguing. In order for one to conclude that Jesus was born on December 25 (for example), one must make four assumptions. First, we must grant that God chooses significant dates to intervene in human history. Second, we must grant that Jesus's conception and death took place on the same date. Third, we must grant that March 25 is in fact the date that Jesus was crucified (which is disputed

---

* Some Christians within the Armenian Church continue to celebrate Christmas on January 6.

among historians). Fourth, we must grant that Jesus's gestation period was exactly nine calendar months.

From the modern historian's perspective, we must conclude that we haven't the first clue of Jesus's birthdate. Rather, December 25 is a theological guess that was not widely commemorated until the sixth century. It wasn't until the year 1038 that the phrase "Mass of Christ" is first attested in Old English (*Cristes Maesse*). This explains how the name "Christmas" evolved. Today, Christians accept the standard date of Christmas without much inquiry.

What is important for the topic of this book, however, is the recognition that commemorating the life of Jesus restructured how Christians thought about their annual calendar. Conversely, once a commemorative calendar had been established, these traditions eventually restructured how Christians thought about Jesus. A theological cycle of interpretation had been established, and Jesus was an integral part of it.

Christ Pantocrator (circa sixth and thirteenth centuries)

From the time Constantine established Constantinople (modern-day Istanbul) as the capital of the Empire (330 CE), to the reign of Justinian (526 CE), the city had steadily grown. By the sixth century it was the most magnificent city in Europe. Art and architecture flourished. Religions and politics found their seats of power there. Constantinople boasted half a million people and the newly built Hagia Sophia. Until 1453, when the Ottomans took the city, Constantinople was the capital of the Byzantine Empire and therefore the capital of Christianity.

One of the major cultural features of this period was its use of religious icons. Two of the greatest iconographic portraits of Jesus stand as virtual bookends of the Byzantine Empire. Both take the form of the "Pantocrator" (meaning all-powerful). Christ, conveying heavenly power, extends his right hand to form a symbolic blessing. The first bookend is the Christ Pantocrator of St Catherine's Monastery at Sinai (Egypt). The fact that Justinian founded the monastery suggests that this encaustic (wax) painting was produced in Constantinople, circa sixth century. It is also possible that an artist of another region was influenced by the work being done in the great city.

Figure 19 Pantocrator of St Catherine's Monastery (circa sixth century).

Famously, the Pantocrator (below) icon portrays duality. The right side of Jesus's face is different from the left in the following ways: shaded darker, higher ear, higher cheekbone, pointed brow, larger eye, less exposed shoulder, arm firmly gripping a tome. Many art historians agree that the right side suggests Christ's human nature, while the left suggests his divine nature. With his divine side, Jesus gestures a blessing. While it might be difficult to see with the untrained eye, his fingers form the Greek letters ICXC, the key characters in his title: IHCOYC XPICTOC. This

Figure 20 Pantocrator of the Hagia Sophia (circa 1261 CE).

is what "Jesus Christ" looks like in Greek, using all capital letters. The first and last letters of these two words are ICXC. In Eastern Christianity during this period, these four letters were commonly used as a reference to Jesus.

Figure 20 represents the second bookend. This image of Christ Pantocrator is dated 1261 CE and adorns the Hagia Sophia in modern-day Istanbul. While the duality theme is less pronounced, it shares several other features in common with Figure 19. And although his hand of blessing is more difficult to discern, the Greek letters IC and XC are displayed prominently on either side of Christ's head. (In the West, Jesus's hand of blessing takes a different form using different fingers.) The tome held by Jesus is almost identical to its St Catherine's counterpart above.

Variations of the Christ Pantocrator can be found in churches and cathedrals all over the world. The image serves as the continuing legacy of the Byzantine Empire and her capital city.

Jesus's portrait in Islam (seventh century)

The legacy of the Prophet Muhammad (circa 570–632 CE) marks the beginning of Islam. The Prophet is credited as writing the Qur'an in the early seventh century (tradition specifies the year 610 CE) by taking dictation from the angel Gabriel. Jesus is mentioned favorably in the Qur'an. While we should not overstate the importance of Christology to Islamic belief, Islamic scripture offers an interesting portrait of Jesus.

Jesus is depicted as a miracle worker and a prophet in Islamic tradition. This much is in keeping with Christian tradition. But Jesus is not portrayed as the "Son of God" as most forms of Christianity taught. Rather, Jesus is called "son of Mary." Jesus was much like Moses in that he was a man given a particular prophetic mission. Indeed, Jesus fits into the Muslim belief that every prophet sent by Allah was sent for the same purpose and with the same message. Unfortunately, humanity continued to corrupt this message and so Allah continued to send prophets (like Moses and Jesus) until Mohammad's perfected message. Thus the Qur'an held Jesus in high esteem, but refused to adopt Christianity's notion of his unique status of "Son" (viz. the doctrine of the Trinity).

An example of this portrait is found in the Qur'an's teaching on Mary's conception. Jesus's birth was thought to be the result of divine intervention:

> the angels said, "O Mary, indeed Allah gives you good tidings of a word from Him, whose name will be the Messiah, Jesus, the son of Mary – distinguished in this world and the Hereafter and among those brought near [to Allah]. He will speak to the people in the cradle and in maturity and will be of the righteous." She said, "My Lord, how will I have a child when no man has touched me?" [The angel] said, "Such is Allah; He creates what He wills. When He decrees a matter, He only says to it, 'Be,' and it is. And He will teach him writing and wisdom and the Torah and the Gospel. And [make him] a messenger to the Children of Israel, [who will say], 'Indeed I have come to you with a sign from your Lord in that I design for you from clay [that which is] like the form of a bird, then I breathe into it and it becomes a bird by permission of Allah. And I cure the blind and the leper, and I give life to the dead by permission of Allah. And I inform you of what you eat and what you store in your houses. Indeed in that is a sign for you, if you are believers. (3:45–9; Surat ʿĀli ʿImrān)

The Qur'an also offers a corrective to the Christian teaching that God is both three and one (i.e. belief in the Trinity: the Father, the Son, and the Holy Spirit):

> O People of the Scripture, do not commit excess in your religion or
> say about Allah except the truth. The Messiah, Jesus, the son of Mary,
> was but a messenger of Allah and His word which He directed to
> Mary and a soul [created at a command] from Him. So believe in Allah
> and His messengers. And do not say, "Three"; desist – it is better for
> you. Indeed, Allah is but one God. Exalted is He above having a son.
> To Him belongs whatever is in the heavens and whatever is on the
> earth. And sufficient is Allah as Disposer of affairs. (4:171; Sūrat l-nisāa)

Another important difference between Christian and Islamic
tradition concerns Jesus's supposed crucifixion. While the crucifixion was central to Christian history and doctrine, the Qur'an
teaches that Jesus was not crucified. Rather, "Allah raised him
to Himself" (4:158) while another who looked like Jesus was
crucified. It is unclear, according to this view, whether Jesus died
and then ascended to Allah, or if Jesus ascended to Allah without
experiencing death.

The Qur'an refers to the name "Jesus" sixteen times and the
title "messiah" ten times. But Jesus in Islamic oral tradition also
refers to Jesus. In the *ḥadīth* (collections of tradition concerning
the stories, teachings, and interpretations of holy men) this saying
is attributed to Jesus:

> Jesus struck the ground with his hand and took up some of it and
> spread it out, and behold, he had gold in one of his hands and clay
> in the other. Then he said to his companions, "Which of them is
> sweeter to your hearts?" They said, "The gold." He said, "They are
> both alike to me."*

While Jesus's escape from crucifixion might not convince historians, this saying confirms two facts about Jesus's ethics. First, asking

---

* Translation from Robson, J., *Christ in Islam* (Lampeter: Llanerch,
1995 [orig. 1929]), p. 77. These collections were probably not compiled
until after the seventh century.

which – gold or clay – is "sweeter to your hearts" coheres with Jesus's concern for the human interior (i.e. intentions, motives, inclinations). Second, Jesus suggests that the pursuit of wealth is valueless, perhaps also encouraging his disciples to avoid such pursuits. Both of these characteristics reveal key elements of historical Jesus research.

The Heliand poem (ninth century)

From the sixth century to the end of the twelfth, Christian missionaries traveled to northern Europe seeking converts. These efforts sometimes included forced conversions. But what was even more common during this period was the subtle way that Christian theology saturated European cultures. Christianity was adapted to ancient traditions, myths, and worldviews. In turn, such "pre-Christian" cultural elements were transformed from the inside out. As Christianity continued to seep into the cracks of European culture (circa 830 CE), the story of Jesus was put into the language of the Saxons in the form of the *Heliand*.

The *Heliand* (meaning "savior") is an epic-style poem that was composed in what we now consider the north of Germany. It harmonizes the diverging narratives of Matthew, Mark, Luke, and John into one, much like Tatian's *Diatessaron* (for more on that, see page 80), hinging largely on John's sequence of Jesus's life.

Many Saxons had been forced to convert during the era of Charlemagne (circa 742–814) and – not surprisingly – remained hostile to the teachings of the Church. Though Christ was now "Lord," many still revered the deity Wōden (Odin). In short, Christianity still represented a foreign culture and ideology. The *Heliand*, therefore, provided the Church with an evangelistic tool in Old Saxon to win local hearts and minds.

The *Heliand* demonstrates a merger of Christianity and a culture that idealized battle and lionized warriors. In clans where nobility required loyalty to a victorious chieftain, Jesus evolved into a "mighty leader" (*mahtig drohtin*). The *Heliand* calls Jesus's disciples "warrior-companions" (*gisidi*); and in aiming to render Jesus as a lionized savior Saxons would worship, the poem extols the idealized follower of Christ as a "warrior-companion" (*gesith*). Warrior-companions, in this culture, were bodyguards. Historian G.R. Murphy explains that warrior-companions were "personally chosen by a ruling chieftain."[*]

In this context, if the poet wanted to praise a people as virtuous their prowess on the battlefield would be aggrandized. For example, here is how the poet explains Jesus's Roman setting:

> At that time the Christian God granted to the Roman people the greatest kingdom. He strengthened the heart of their army so that they had conquered every nation. Those helmet-lovers from hillfort Rome had won an empire… In Jerusalem, Herod was chosen to be king over the Jewish people. Caesar, ruling the empire from hill-fort Rome, placed him there – among the warrior-companions – even though Herod did not belong by clan to the noble and well-born descendants of Israel.[**]

In explaining Jesus's kinsmen, the poet refers to "the descendants of Israel, those fighting men renowned for their toughness."

Jesus, then, is made from stern stuff. Indeed, Jesus is the "Ruler" and "the most powerful Person ever born." But Jesus must also confront formidable opponents in Rome, and the Jewish leaders:

---

[*] Murphy, G.R., *The Heliand: The Saxon Gospel*. (Oxford: Oxford University Press, 1992), p. 5.
[**] Murphy, *Heliand*, p. 5.

He asked His good followers, the twelve, to come closer – they were the most loyal men on earth to Him – and told them one more time what hardships lay before Him. "And there can be no doubt about it," He said. He said that they should journey to Jerusalem, to the Jewish people. "There everything will come to pass, it will happen among that people, just as wise men said about Me long ago in their words. There, among that powerful people, warrior-heroes will sell me to the leaders."… "They will subject Me to unbelievable torture with the weapon's edge. They will take My life. I will rise up from death and come back to this light by the Chieftain's power, on the third day."*

God (thought to be the "Christian God") is called "the Chieftain." Both Jesus's followers and the Jews of Jerusalem are called warriors. We also see the germinating seeds of anti-Semitism: "Then He traveled onward – He wanted to go to Jerusalem to teach the Jewish people happiness. He was very well aware of their attitude of ill-will, grim hatred and deep hostility."** In this portrait, Jesus is painted as a happy warrior-poet, while the warrior-heroes of Jerusalem are hateful and hostile. The poet follows the formula of Germanic hero epics by casting Jesus as the loyal and generous hero who must confront disloyal and greedy enemies.

Of course, the marriage of Christianity to warrior ethics is at least as old as Constantine the Great (272–337 CE). This poem only provides a snapshot of how Jesus was appropriated in one particular European setting. But granting that Christianity was on the cusp of the first crusades – the first was a massacre of the Jews of Rhineland in 1096 – the popularity of the *Heliand* during this period reveals an important episode in the evolution of Jesus's legacy.

---

* *Heliand,* p. 115.
** *Heliand,* p. 115.

Ultimately, and perhaps ironically, this transformation of Jesus does not result in a change of his crucifixion. Jesus is still executed in the end and rises "back to this light by the Chieftain's power." Thus Jesus's courage is demonstrated in an unexpected way, despite being cast as a mighty leader of warrior-companions.

Clare of Assisi (thirteenth century)

Clare of Assisi is best known for following Francis of Assisi into monastic living and establishing the female branch of the Franciscan order. Her life also attests to an important development in how Jesus was imagined among those who took vows of poverty.

Taking a vow of poverty was paramount for both Clare and Francis. Both grew up in wealthy households and gave up considerable comfort because they believed that this was the way that Jesus lived. They believed that living apart from wealth and comfort was a way to be closer to Christ. In this context, Jesus's status as divine "groom" became important.

MEET THIS WORD: ROMANCE

Romance derives from the Old French *romanz*, meaning "verse narrative." In the thirteenth century, the word referred to the story of a hero or knight. A century later, the word had the sense of recitation of stories into French. These verses – often sung dramatically by troubadours to wealthy women – became a popular way to express affection. But it wasn't until the seventeenth century that Romance referred specifically to a "love story." In the early twentieth century, the term was used in reference to "a love affair" (eschewing the sense of adventure in the heroic sense). The word can now refer to a group of languages, a sense of adventure, or courtly love.

In his youth, Francis was enamored with the love poetry of the troubadours. Prior to these traveling love poets, most wealthy Europeans married for security and progeny as arranged by their parents. But the world was changing. In the time of the troubadours wealthy women began to imagine a different kind of marriage; it was now possible to choose a spouse based on romantic love.* Song writers would croon and swoon as they expressed their love for a wealthy woman at court (hence the term "courtship"). This fashion took centuries to become common practice, but Francis was among the first generation to be caught up in love poetry as a life ethic.

Francis, however, had a problem. A devoted man of religion was expected to demonstrate his devotion by going to war against infidels. Thus, Francis was among the many Christian warriors of the crusades during this period. This was the setting for Francis's religious experience. As the story goes, he received a vision that changed his life. He was convinced that he had been called to a life of peace and simplicity, so he left the battlefield and went home. Francis became sullen and insular. Finally, he abandoned all of his wealth and became a traveling preacher. This is when he met Clare.

Francis described his new devotion to Jesus as his marriage to a "woman of surpassing beauty", and named his new bride Lady Poverty. His devotion to Christ was a metaphorical marriage to an ideal. Influenced by his time with the troubadours, Francis described his religious life as a love story. Clare, having heard Francis preach, was wooed to the monastic life too. In adopting her new life ethic, Clare was "married to Christ." Jesus was her groom.

---

* For more on the shift to marriage practices initiated by courtly love (i.e. romance), see Le Donne, A., *The Wife of Jesus: Ancient Texts and Modern Scandals* (London: Oneworld, 2013), ch. 6.

In a letter she penned shortly before her death, Clare wrote of her groom as one "whose beauty all the heavenly hosts admire unceasingly; whose love inflames our love." She explains:

> Inasmuch as this vision is the splendor of eternal glory, the brilliance of eternal life and the mirror without blemish, look upon that mirror each day, O queen and spouse of Jesus Christ, and continually within it, so that you may adorn yourself within and without with beautiful robes and cover yourself with the flowers and garments of all the virtues as becomes the daughter and most chaste bride of the Most High King.[*]

Clare instructs the devoted follower of Jesus to imagine herself as a bride on her wedding day. A life devoted to Jesus is like receiving a vision of the perfect, royal marriage. Looking at this vision is like a "mirror without blemish" revealing one's outer and inner beauty. Jesus, in this vision, is not only the groom; he is the author of the vision that makes the bride see herself as beautiful.

The Letter of Lentulus (circa fourteenth and fifteenth centuries)

The Letter of Lentulus is a fictional letter attributed to a fictional politician called Publius Lentulus. It purports to offer a physical description of Jesus from a Roman eyewitness. The letter was circulated in Latin in the fifteenth century, but might be much older.

> Lentulus, the Governor of the Jerusalemites to the Roman Senate and People, greetings. There has appeared in our times, and there still lives, a man of great power (virtue), called Jesus Christ. The people

---

[*] Translation from Armstrong, R.J. and Brady, I., *Francis and Clare: The Complete Works* (New York: Paulist Press, 1982), p. 204.

call him prophet of truth; his disciples, son of God. He raises the dead, and heals infirmities. He is a man of medium size; he has a venerable aspect, and his beholders can both fear and love him. His hair is of the colour of the ripe hazelnut, straight down to the ears, but below the ears wavy and curled, with a bluish and bright reflection, flowing over his shoulders. It is parted in two on the top of the head, after the pattern of the Nazarenes. His brow is smooth and vary [sic] cheerful with a face without wrinkle or spot, embellished by a slightly reddish complexion. His nose and mouth are faultless. His beard is abundant, of the colour of his hair, not long, but divided at the chin. His aspect is simple and mature, his eyes are changeable and bright. He is terrible in his reprimands, sweet and amiable in his admonitions, cheerful without loss of gravity. He was never known to laugh, but often to weep. His stature is straight, his hands and arms beautiful to behold. His conversation is grave, infrequent, and modest. He is the most beautiful among the children of men.*

This fictional account of Jesus's appearance seems to have influenced many European artists. Or, perhaps, it simply reinforced their European imaginations. This Jesus has long, straight, hazelnut hair, a full beard and a blemish-free reddish complexion. Clearly this fictionalized portrait of Jesus is European. The fact that this Jesus is grave and "never known to laugh" fits well with most depictions of him in art history.

The mention of Jesus's medium height, faultless complexion and bright eyes are clues to why Jesus is described at all. These are telltale markers of the philosophy of "physiognomy." Physiognomic description is an ancient Greek and Roman way to explain a person's character by interpreting their physique and facial features. Comparisons with animals are common in these descriptions. Moderate height is seen as a virtue. Indeed, almost all moderation is seen as virtuous. Noticeable flaws would include

---

* "Pribius Lentulus," *Catholic Encyclopedia*. [Online]. (URL http://www.newadvent.org/cathen/09154a.htm). (Accessed March 29, 2018).

being too tall or too short, too hairy or too bald, too doe-eyed or too beady-eyed. Such characteristics would reveal character flaws. Jesus's face is "without wrinkle or spot," perhaps owing to the metaphor of Jesus as the spotless "lamb" of God ("like that of a lamb without defect or blemish", 1 Pet. 1:19). The zoological association is not explicit in the letter. It would, however, fit with the other obvious physiognomic features.

Most importantly, a man's eyes are windows into his soul. So it is crucial to note that the author of this letter is not simply suggest-ing what Jesus looked like, he is much more concerned with Jesus's character: he has power, is a man of truth, is both loved and feared. Jesus is cheerful but grave (i.e. moderate in demeanor). He stands up straight and possesses a quiet beauty. Notice also that his complex-ion is ruddy, but only slightly so. When measured by the standards of physiognomy, these features reveal Jesus's virtuous temperance.

Finally, three points are important. First, much of Western art propels this fiction. Second, contrary to this fiction, Jesus is depicted in the gospels as a man of extremes. His words were nei-ther "infrequent" nor "modest." Jesus was an argumentative man and, at times verbose, according to our earliest sources. Third, and most important, contrary to the European imagination, we would do better to imagine Jesus as a native of the Middle-Eastern world.

Jesus and the human form (fifteenth and sixteenth centuries)

The early Italian Renaissance (beginning from the early thir-teenth century) emerged from a highly religious setting. Scenes from Jesus's life were pervasive during this period. Artists returned to the topic repeatedly. Concurrently, the period was a revolution in the study of human anatomy and the use of perspective. By developing techniques to accurately depict the anatomy of Jesus, Italian painters began to master the human form.

The study of human anatomy by artists and scientists alike often involved the examination of human corpses. By analyzing the musculature and structure of the human body, artists were able to replicate the shapes of their study to express volume. Andrea Mantegna showcases artistic developments in perspective, volume, and anatomy in this tempera masterpiece entitled, the *Lamentation over the Dead Christ* (late fifteenth century).

Here, the post-crucifixion corpse is Jesus. The volume and light expressed on Jesus's torso will become a key interest of later

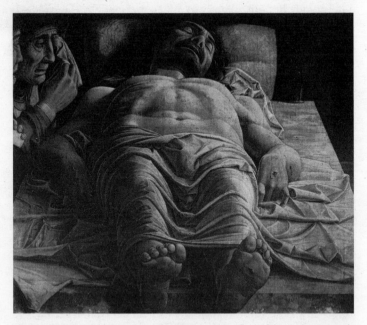

Figure 21 *Lamentation over the Dead Christ* (late fifteenth century): Tempera on canvas by Andrea Mantegna

Renaissance artists as well. Mantegna's attention to anatomical detail in the feet alone is superb. Moreover, who imagined – until now – the subject of the crucifixion from this perspective? Jesus's pierced feet become the scene's entry point.

It should be said, however, that Mantegna imagines Jesus's pierced hands with anachronism. Constantine had outlawed the practice of crucifixion centuries earlier. By the fifteenth century, few people knew that the practice required the nailing of fore-arms below the wrists. Thus Mantegna repeats the error of many

Figure 22: Michelangelo's *Pietà* (circa 1499): Sculpted from Carrara marble, it is displayed in Saint Peter's Basilica (Vatican City). A pietà is a common theme in depictions of Mary, the mother of Jesus, in which Mary holds the dead body of her son.

other artists. Because the pre-Constantine portraits of Jesus did not depict Jesus with realistic details, the artists of the Renaissance had to mine their own imagination for such details.

Few artists of the high Italian Renaissance are more celebrated than Raphael. His fresco, *The School of Athens*, in the Vatican marks a highlight of the period. The oil painting in figure 23 of Jesus's resurrection (early sixteenth century) is one of the earliest of Raphael's works.

Figure 23 *Resurrection of Christ* (early sixteenth century).

Jesus's torso, while understated, benefits from a study of musculature and his statuesque pose recalls classical Greek and Roman sculptures. Artists of this period endeavored to convey a range of human emotions, postures, and actions. Episodes from Jesus's life provided a way to demonstrate a complex drama within a single scene and Raphael's resurrection is a case in point.

Jesus is serene, almost disaffected. He is perhaps more a creature of heaven at this point as his head extends higher than the accompanying angels. The Roman guards are confused, staggering backward. But they all raise one arm skyward as if to showcase the miracle unwittingly. Three women, all bearing saintly halos, are looking down. Perhaps this suggests that they are not yet aware of what they will encounter at the empty sarcophagus. Artists of this period built from their mastery of the human form and added a study of the human condition.

Another word on these Italian artists is warranted: they are recreating religious narratives with visual media. In their narratives, Jesus is unmistakably European. His pale skin and hazelnut hair help to create the assumption of Jesus's whiteness that will plague the modern era.

Conclusion

Even with a cursory glance at the depictions of Jesus from the third to fifteenth centuries, we see that he was made and remade into the image of those commemorating him. Jesus, then, remains an important window into cultural memories. We can see the ideals, the aspirations, the assumptions, and the prejudices of his commemorators by analyzing Jesus's evolution. By analyzing Jesus's portrayal in stories, texts, paintings, and sculptures, we witness snapshots of north African, west Asian, and European imaginations.

Each portrait and narrative of Jesus requires critique. Most incarnations of Jesus do not cohere with Jesus as a figure in history. In such cases, we must ask why. *Why did the storyteller choose to cast Jesus in this light? Why did the artist portray Jesus in this way? What are the cultural assumptions of this theologian?* I hope that such questions will hinder us from accepting cultural biases unwittingly.

Most importantly, in analyzing Jesus in art, theology, and storytelling, we gain the opportunity to critique ourselves. Surely we have cultural biases that we cannot see. If some of the greatest minds of the past two thousand years projected themselves into Jesus's portraiture, then we too are not immune. Finally, part of being self-aware is being honest with ourselves about our limitations. In our attempt to critique a cultural portrait of Jesus, are we too eager to find fault? Do we have a tendency to be over critical at times? When it comes to Jesus, we are never neutral observers.

Five books about Jesus in the premodern imagination

Anatolios, K. *Retrieving Nicaea: The Development and Meaning of Trinitarian Doctrine.* (Grand Rapids: Baker Academic, 2011).

Brakke, D. *The Gnostics: Myth, Ritual, and Diversity in Early Christianity.* (Reprint edn; Cambridge: Harvard University Press, 2012).

Levering, M. *The Theology of Augustine: An Introductory Guide to His Most Important Works.* (Grand Rapids: Baker Academic, 2013).

Pelikan, J. *The Illustrated Jesus Through the Centuries.* (New Haven: Yale University Press, 1997).

Schäfer, P. *Jesus in the Talmud* (Princeton: Princeton University Press, 2009).

4

Jesus in modern intelligentsia

"But the greatest of all the reformers of the depraved religion of His own country was Jesus of Nazareth. Abstracting what is really His from the rubbish in which he is buried, easily distinguished by its luster from the dross of His biographers, and as separable from that as the diamond from the dunghill, we have the outlines of a system of the most sublime morality which has ever fallen from the lips of man; outlines which it is lamentable He did not live to fill up."

Thomas Jefferson

An intellectual puzzle

If the story of the medieval Western world is religious expansion, the story of the modern era is intellectual exploration. Again, there is no single timeline to follow. We witness, rather, a gnarled vineyard of intellectual growth. Intellectual culture can be knotted, meandering, and backtracking. It is branching, spiraling, and overlapping. There are seasons of green, and years without rain. For every season, a new Jesus emerges.

The modern era witnessed the invention of Jesus, the enlightened genius.* Jesus was cast as the Aryan "destroyer of Judaism." Others saw him as an observant Jew who brought religion to the Gentiles. Jesus became a prototype for the modern ethicist. He served as a precedent for Mormonite plural marriage. Jesus the would-be militant revolutionary was entertained and dismissed. Eventually, Jesus as end-times prophet re-emerged.

Jesus continued to fascinate the best and the brightest minds. Some of the most creative portraits come from philosophers who are known for work in other areas. Politicians, poets, and polymaths weighed in. They turned to the gospels from their usual pursuits and looked for the real Jesus by reading between the lines. Some would look for a few elements of the gospels to lift from the story and construct a new history.

This period also widened the rift between the common Sunday worshiper of Jesus – the Christ you learn about in hymns – and the ivory-tower elites. Most Christians are not interested in this sort of historical reconstruction, but they are generally interested in new and creative ways to express their relationship to Jesus. On this front, the modern period continued for most Christians just as it had before; but seeds of dissent were planted foreshadowing a mass exodus from usual worship in the Western world in the twentieth century. In this chapter I will survey some of the intellectual creativity of the modern era. It must be kept in mind, however, that many intellectuals (alongside regular folk) remained quite confident in the biblical portraits of Jesus. Most people were – and are – unmoved by scholarly reconstructions of Jesus's life.

---

* There is some dispute about when the so-called "modern era" began. I begin this section with the life of Baruch (Benedict) Spinoza, which is from 1632–77. Some would see Spinoza as a precursor to the modern period.

MEET THESE WORDS: DEISM, THEISM, PANTHEISM

"Deism" comes from the French *déisme*, which borrows from the Latin *deus*, meaning "god." Deism reflects a seventeenth-century trend in philosophy to distance the European concept of a relational god from the natural world. In this philosophy, the Creator does not interact with the natural world. The traditional view of the Abrahamic faiths was then relabeled "theism." This word borrows from the Greek *theos*, meaning "God." In the early eighteenth century, the term "pantheism" (borrowing from the Greek prefix *pan-*, meaning "all") was coined to label the view that God and the universe are one and the same.

A key characteristic of this period is the rejection of supernatural stories. Those influenced by German historiography and English deism could no longer read the gospels as historical documents. If a story conveyed a miracle, the most natural solution was to label it mythological, rather than historical. David Friedrich Strauss (1835) wrote: "It is not by any means meant that the whole history of Jesus is to be represented as mythical, but only that every part of it is to be subjected to a critical examination, to ascertain whether it have not some admixture of the mythical."* Jesus as a figure in history required critical examination by professional historians. The English translation of Strauss's book (completed by novelist George Eliot) was titled, *The Life of Jesus Critically Examined*. According to Strauss, the German people needed a Jesus who was not packaged in myth. Each element of his life must be examined scientifically and critically.

While these critics had little (or no) confidence in accounts of the supernatural, they were perhaps overconfident in their ability to discover and analyze Jesus's psychological makeup. Strauss praised Theodor Keim for his "divination" into the psychology

---

* Strauss, D.F., *The Life of Jesus Critically Examined*, trans. George Eliot (4th edn; London: Swan Sonnenschein & Co., 1902), p. xxix.

and mental states of Jesus. But a similar description could be used of several of the biographies of Jesus during this period. Keim charted "the psychological development of the messianic consciousness of Jesus out of inward experiences and outward impressions and impulses." Keim's biography, according to Strauss, "is an able and suggestive effort to penetrate, as far as the state of the sources admits, by means of sympathetic and reproductive divination, to the personal experiences and mental states of the religious genius from whom a new epoch in the world's religious history proceeded."*

Strauss's praise of Keim gives a window into three important elements of the modern era. First, Jesus's psychology became an interesting topic. Second, many philosophers measured history in epochs launched by great geniuses. Third, Jesus was exactly this sort of genius. In other words, Jesus was not a man for his own time, but a man for the era that was dawning.**

The "historical Jesus" was no longer the property of the Church. In many cases, historians reconstructed Jesus as a historical figure in order to deconstruct Christianity's pious portraits of him. The new common sense was that the gospels are not trustworthy as historical documents. Once determined untrustworthy, Jesus became even more malleable. Historians – like all artists who look to Jesus – shaped Jesus into their own likeness or into the likeness of the institutions they detested.

But some of these iconoclasts worried about the damage they might cause to the faith. Hermann Samuel Reimarus chose not to publish his reconstruction of the historical Jesus. Strauss wrote that he was "aware that the essence of the Christian faith is perfectly independent of [my] criticism. The supernatural birth of Christ, his miracles his resurrection and ascension, remain eternal

---

* Strauss, *Life of Jesus*, p. xxiv.
** There is an implicit anti-Judaism in this view of Jesus. More on this from p. 152.

truths, whatever doubts may be cast on their reality as historical facts."*

There was a growing worry that the "Jesus of history" could not be reconciled to the "Christ of faith." But what both Jesus and Christ shared in common was their persistence in cultural reconstruction. The difference between the two identities became a popular intellectual puzzle: *How do we explain how Jesus (the man) turned into Christ (the institutional symbol)?* In solving this puzzle, historians projected something of themselves onto the task. Nobel Laureate, Albert Schweitzer, wrote that "each individual created him in accordance with his own character." Accordingly, "There is no historical task which so reveals a man's true self as the writing of a Life of Jesus. No vital force comes into the figure unless a man breathes into it all the hate or all the love of which he is capable."**

Spinoza: The mind of Christ (seventeenth century)

One of the finest minds of the early modern period was that of Baruch (Benedict) Spinoza. Spinoza had been expelled from Judaism due to his theological views. His understanding of God is notoriously difficult to summarize, but he seems to have merged pantheism and theism in his thought. Spinoza blurred the distinction between Creator and nature. In his *Tractatus Theologico-Politicus* (*TTP*), published posthumously in 1677, he turns his attention to the God of the Bible and argues that the human mind is incapable of encountering and comprehending

---

* Strauss, *Life of Jesus*, p. xxx.
** Schweitzer, A., *The Quest of the Historical Jesus: A Critical Study of Its Progress From Reimarus to Wrede*, trans. W. Montgomery (Mineola, N.Y.: Dover, 2005), p. 4.

God's voice without tainting it with imagination and emotional inclination:

> We may be able quite to comprehend that God can communicate immediately with man, for without the intervention of bodily means He communicates to our minds His essence; still, a man who can by pure intuition comprehend ideas which are neither contained in nor deducible from the foundations of our natural knowledge, must necessarily possess a mind far superior to those of his fellow men, nor do I believe that any have been so endowed save Christ. (*TTP* 1.47)

The human mind, he argues is too limited to commune directly with the mind of God. But Spinoza's one exception to this rule is Christ. Jesus, from this view, had a mind superior to all others (only finding competition with Moses, as his treatment of Moses suggests). Spinoza turned his attention to the vocation of prophets, as it was their job to relate the mind of God to humanity. In his view, the prophetic ability to comprehend the mind of God was limited. But while most prophets could only imagine the voice of God, and thus distort their experience of the divine, Jesus's mind was different:

> To [Christ] the ordinances of God leading men to salvation were revealed directly without words or visions, so that God manifested Himself to the Apostles through the mind of Christ as He formerly did to Moses through the supernatural voice. In this sense the voice of Christ, like the voice which Moses heard, may be called the voice of God, and it may be said that the wisdom of God (i.e. wisdom more than human) took upon itself in Christ human nature, and that Christ was the way of salvation...it follows that if Moses spoke with God face to face as a man speaks with his friend (i.e. by means of their two bodies) Christ communed with God mind to mind. Thus we may conclude that no one except Christ received the revelations of God without the aid of imagination, whether in words or vision. (*TTP* 1.48–9, 51–2)

While Spinoza seems to be praising Jesus, he is at the same time dismissing Christianity. Spinoza continues to explain that Jesus had to package his divine thoughts in the language categories used by his disciples. Spinoza argued that whatever Jesus taught, his followers must have misunderstood. Likewise, God may have spoken with Moses person-to-person, but who among the prophets was able to accurately comprehend Moses? God may have communed with Christ mind-to-mind, but who among the disciples was able to accurately translate the mind of Christ into doctrine? Simply put, the human mind was incapable of fully grasping the mind of God. Therefore, Spinoza writes, "I must at this juncture declare that those doctrines which certain churches put forward concerning Christ, I neither affirm nor deny, for I freely confess that I do not understand them" (*TTP* 1:50).

This line of reasoning will take many forms in the modern era. The implication is that the doctrines of the Church do not hold a monopoly on the mind of God. Perhaps, then, a better way to commune with God is through the natural world and through logic. Once the authority of the Church had been undermined, reason and argumentation had been empowered. Freedom of thought was a key element of the European Enlightenment that followed.

Reimarus: Jesus as failed king (eighteenth century)

The fault lines between the "Jesus of history" and the "Christ of faith" began to crack when H.S. Reimarus died. The Professor of Hebrew and Oriental Languages at the Hamburg Gymnasium, Germany, died on 1 March, 1768. Hermann Samuel Reimarus had been educated in theology, but studied widely as a professor. He was interested in natural history, economics, and mathematics, but was best known for his study and collected translations of Cassius Dio (an ancient Roman author). As a philosopher, he published on logic.

But Reimarus had a secret.

His secret – which only a few knew until after his death – was his alternative history of Jesus's life and fate. Very few people knew that Reimarus harbored what would have been considered heresy. Family friend and colleague, Gotthold Lessing, began circulating some of Reimarus's previously unpublished writings after his death. Lessing called them *Fragments by an Anonymous Writer*, and controversy followed.

Reimarus created his alternative history by reading between the lines of the gospels. The basic thesis was that Jesus was a political revolutionary in life, a failure in death, and a fraud in his afterlife. Jesus saw himself as a political savior who intended to be king. His aspirations got him executed on a Roman cross. Jesus, according to Reimarus, had promised deliverance and went to Jerusalem to start a rebellion. His violent demonstration within the Temple precincts was meant to start a riot and then a rebellion. Rome, of course, ended this rebellion before it began. His disciples robbed the tomb and created a false narrative of his resurrection. The reports of miracles too could not be trusted. This view was consistent with deism (i.e. God is not involved in human affairs), which was popular during this period. Jesus, therefore, had been misunderstood by the Church because the Church had trusted in the gospels, which were untrustworthy.

In a letter to a friend, Reimarus confessed that he wrote his alternative history of Jesus to calm himself. He had long been troubled by doubt, but decided to confront the matter head on. So Reimarus used his research to help him decide for himself whether his doubts were well founded. Lessing – who championed Reimarus's alternative history – was struggling with similar doubts. Once Reimarus had passed, Lessing used the publication of Reimarus's *Fragments* as a way to deal with his own faith crisis. Two friends – Christoph F.

Nicolai and Moses Mendelssohn – who knew of Lessing's intentions to publish begged him to keep the secret. But Lessing was determined to work out his doubts in public.

We see in both Reimarus and Lessing the conflict created when the theism of Christianity (the prevailing view of Christendom) clashes with the deism of the Enlightenment

Figure 24 *Bavarian Good Shepherd* (circa 1750): This painting by an unknown Bavarian artist is an Aryan iteration of the Good Shepherd. Both the hat and the landscape place the theme in the artist's geographical setting. Jesus is depicted with pink skin and European phenotypes.

(a trend among European intelligentsia). In this case, the topic of Jesus became a worktable to confront this conflict and thus work out a faith crisis.

Reimarus's alternative history of Jesus became a prototype for a new, dedicated field of study: historical Jesus research. In the following centuries, this field of study produced hundreds of Jesus biographies and critical deconstructions of the New Testament. The field began to measure Jesus against the politics of his day and situate him within a historical – not a theological – setting.

Emden: A Jew for the Gentiles (eighteenth century)

Rabbi Jacob Emden of Altona (1697–1776) was one of the most respected Torah scholars of the modern era. Emden received letters from scholars all over Europe asking him for advice. Moses Mendelssohn – philosopher and polymath – once wrote to him calling himself Emden's disciple. Sometimes Rabbi Emden would be called upon to settle disputes.

In the eighteenth century, the Polish rabbinate excommunicated a sect of Jewish Sabbateans led by Jacob Frank. The Sabbateans held that Rabbi Sabbatai Zevi (1626–76) was the Messiah. This belief created a rift between the sect and Judaism at large. The sect responded by accusing the rabbinate of persecution and appealed to the Catholic Church for help. According to the Sabbateans, they had "confessed the Trinity," and this was the reason for their excommunication. (It is unclear why they confessed the Trinity or, conversely, why they would have claimed to do so.) The lamentable result of this appeal was an even worse persecution by local Christians toward the Jews of Podolias (the region of Ukraine that now borders Moldova). The bishop commanded that all copies of the Talmud in the bishopric of Podolias should be burned. The sect, claiming to be converted to Christianity, agreed to be baptized. Rabbi Jacob Emden was sought for advice on the escalating tensions. He was no friend of the Sabbatean movement, but he hoped for a peaceful coexistence between Jews and Christians.

Rabbi Emden believed that the religion founded by Jesus was a moral institution at its roots. (Importantly, he believed that Jesus was indeed the founder of Christianity.) So Emden advised a direct appeal for help from the local Polish clergy. If Jesus was moral, perhaps a moral argument might solve the problem. The Sabbateans were rumored to be "sexual deviants" and thus could not possibly be good Catholics. So, Emden suggested, the Catholic leaders and Jewish leaders had more in common which each other than with the newly converted sect.

To make his point, Rabbi Emden argued that Jesus was born Jewish and kept the laws of Moses (613 laws had been established). Jesus was also determined to create a moral religion for non-Jews. This religion would only require seven laws.* While Jesus "the Nazarene" himself kept all 613 commandments, he unburdened his disciples from this requirement. Emden wrote:

> The Nazarene and his Apostles never meant to abolish the Torah of Moses from one who was born a Jew. Likewise did Paul write in his letter to the Corinthians (1 Cor. 7) that each should adhere to the faith in which each was called. They therefore acted in accordance with the Torah by forbidding circumcision to Gentiles, according to

---

* Jewish tradition that postdates the Bible claims that Noah established seven laws for Gentiles. These seven laws vary depending on the source, but here is one list: All of humankind was expected (1) not to worship idols; (2) not to blaspheme the name of God; (3) to establish courts of justice; (4) not to kill; (5) not to commit adultery; (6) not to rob (7); not to eat flesh that had been cut from a living animal. In the New Testament, Acts 15:20 echoes these requirements for Gentiles by focusing on items one, four, five, and seven.

the Halakha, as it is forbidden to one who does not accept the yoke of the commandments. They knew that it would be too difficult for the Gentiles to observe the Torah of Moses…that the Nazarene brought about a double kindness in the world. On the one hand, he strengthened the Torah of Moses majestically, as mentioned earlier, and not one of our Sages spoke out more emphatically concerning the immutability of the Torah. And on the other hand, he did much good for the Gentiles [non-Jews].*

In Emden's reconstruction, Jesus was a Jew who reached out to non-Jews. It is an inconvenient fact, however, that Jesus in the gospels rarely speaks to Gentiles. But for the Catholics to which Emden appealed, it would have seemed reasonable that Jesus and Paul were working in the same direction: toward Gentile inclusion and toward the establishment of the Roman Catholic Church. In essence, Emden was calling Christians to be good Christians by allowing Jews to be good Jews. Good Christians should "bring their people to love the ancient Children of Israel who remain loyal to their God, as indeed commanded to Christians by their original teachers." He drives home the point:

> They even said to love one's enemies. How much more so to us! In the name of heaven, we are your brothers! One God has created us all. Why should they abuse us because we are joined to the commandments of God, to which we are tied with the ropes of his love? You, members of the Christian faith, how good and pleasant it might be if you will observe that which was commanded to you by your first teachers; how wonderful is your share if you will assist the Jews in the observance of their Torah.

For Emden, Jesus was the bridge between two peoples. Jesus was a champion of peace. While other Enlightenment thinkers were

---

* This segment draws from the work of Falk, H., *Jesus the Pharisee* (Mahwah: Paulist Press, 1985), esp. pp. 13–23. All quotations of Rabbi Emden are his.

driving a wedge between the historical Jesus and the Church, Jacob Emden called for a better adherence of the Church to the teachings of the historical Jesus.

Jefferson: Ethicist for the Americans (nineteenth century)

There are perhaps more brilliant polymaths, more complex characters, and weightier influencers in American history, but Thomas Jefferson (1743–1826) is a near rival, no matter the name. Because of his multifaceted legacy, it is often forgotten that Jefferson was keenly interested in reconstructing Jesus: the ethics of Jesus, to be precise.

Jefferson had a sense that America was giving birth to something new, but needed some sort of moral anchor. In a series of letters, and then by way of literal cutting and pasting, he created his own Bible (although it was not published until after his death). Jefferson's project was to remove the theological packaging of the gospels so that only Jesus's teachings remained. He believed that he was liberating "the most sublime and benevolent code of morals which has ever been offered to man" from the shackles of irrational superstition. And, as the quotation at the beginning of part four of his book suggests, Jefferson also had a low view of Jesus's upbringing within Judaism. He called Judaism the "depraved religion of His own country." I think it is impossible to read these words and not see the force of anti-Semitism behind them.*

---

* Jefferson's relationship with Jews and Judaism is complex as in some ways he was a champion for tolerance in America in the face of anti-Semitism. See more in *Jews in America: Thomas Jefferson and the Jews*. Jewish Virtual Library. [Online]. (URL http://www.jewishvirtuallibrary.org/thomas-jefferson-and-the-jews) (Accessed March 29, 2018).

With the aim to remove both the "depravity" of Judaism and the superstition of Christianity, Jefferson set out to find the authentic ethics of Jesus. The result was an eighty-four-page "Bible" constructed of Jesus's words, but without any supernatural accounts (*c.*1820). He called it *The Life and Morals of Jesus of Nazareth: Extracted Textually from the Gospels in Greek, Latin, French, and English.*

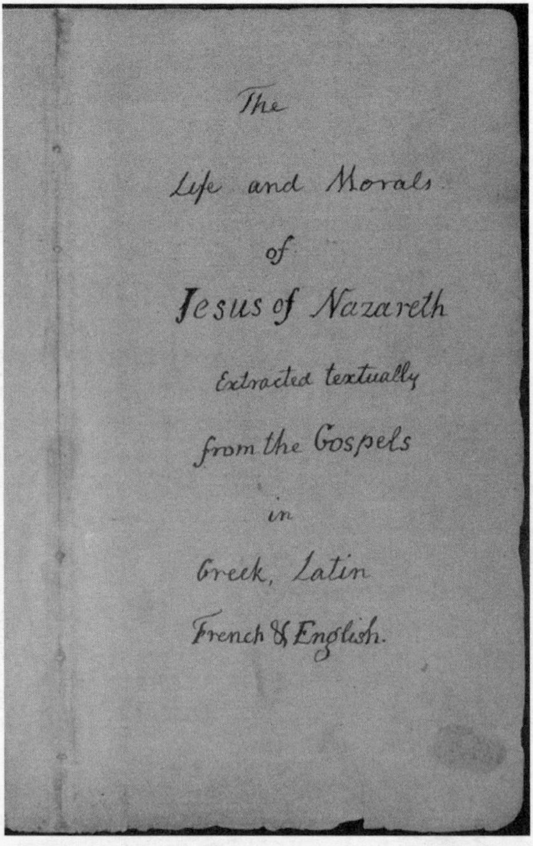

Figure 25 *The Jefferson Bible* (circa 1820).

Jefferson – much like the deists of Europe – had no use for the supernatural. Much like Spinoza before him, Jefferson reconstructed a Jesus that was a prototype for the Enlightenment. Jefferson, to this end, created a physical artifact – a revised Bible – that represented his revision.

Jefferson's Jesus was made by a process of reconstruction. He seemed to have three tools at work for this task:

1. *Analogy*: In Jefferson's case, it is clear that the criterion of analogy was at work. This criterion works from the logic that there are predictable constants in the natural world, both ancient and modern. Thus, if there were no legitimate accounts of resurrections and water-walking in 1820, it stands to reason that there were no such happenings in the first century either.

Figure 26 *Flevit super illam* (meaning "He wept over it") by Enrique Simonet, oil on canvas (1892): It parallels the French Romantic period with an emphasis on emotion and idealized landscape. Simonet is reputed to have left Christianity while he studied art, but returned to Christ as a subject with new eyes after his departure from religion.

2. *Epoch-making genius*: Another factor that influenced Jefferson was a key element of neo-romanticism. Jefferson believed that a great man's genius had the power to create a new epoch in human history. In Jefferson's view, the genius of Jesus had created a new epoch and was worthy of revitalizing alongside the birth of America.

3. *Private religion*: Jefferson's political interests influenced his reconstruction of Jesus. The idea of private religion as tolerated by the state – but not enforced by the state – was important to Jefferson. As such, Jesus became a teacher, not a preacher. Jesus became a guide, not the agent of a divine judge. Jefferson seemingly had no intention for his Bible to be published or widely disseminated. It remained in his private library until his death.

Young: Jesus the polygamist (nineteenth century)

Brigham Young (1801–77) was among the original Mormons, the second president of the movement, and founder of Salt Lake City, Utah. Alongside Joseph Smith, Young established the Church of Jesus Christ of Latter-Day Saints (originally called the "Mormonites"), which now includes over 15 million members.

Before becoming Smith's successor, Young worked beneath Smith in Nauvoo, Illinois. It was in Nauvoo that Smith first introduced the idea of plural marriage. At first, Young was opposed to the idea but changed his view upon receiving a sign from God on the matter. Before Young's death in 1877, he had been "sealed to" as many as fifty-five women.

This sexual ethic was projected onto both God the Father and Jesus. Late in life, Young wrote: "Said [Jesus], when talking to his disciples: 'He that hath seen me hath seen the Father;' and,

'I and my Father are one.' The Scripture says that He, the Lord, came walking in the Temple, with His train; I do not know who they were, unless His wives and children.'*

To understand Young's thought process, one must recognize three steps in his logic. First, Jesus reflects the image of God. Young makes this point quite forcefully with his two citations of John's gospel. Young furthermore believed that the human family unit was a metaphor for God's image. Second, God is literally a father. Quoting the biblical prophet Isaiah, Young suggests that God is married many times over with numerous children: "I saw also the Lord sitting upon a throne, high and lifted up, and his train filled the temple" (Isa. 6:1). In the *King James Bible*, "his train" is a suitably vague translation, allowing Young to suppose that the Lord is followed by his family. (Most other translations say "the *train of his robe* filled the Temple.") Third, Jesus, reflecting divine reality, lived out the virtuous practice of plural marriage. Young writes: "The same truth is borne out by the Savior."**

Seemingly it took years for Young to come to the belief that Jesus practiced plural marriage. As Young's early distaste for the idea indicates, plural marriage was far afield from popular American notions of normalcy. He became a defender of its legitimacy only after being persuaded by Joseph Smith and his religious experience. Young eventually taught, "The only men who become Gods, even Sons of God, are those who enter into polygamy."***

Young persuaded his colleague, Orson Pratt, to take up the argument for polygamy in public. In an 1853 article titled "Celestial Marriage," Orson Pratt argued that Jesus (like his

---

* Young, B., "Gathering the Poor – Religion a Science," *Journal of Discourses*, 13, 1871, pp. 300–9, here p. 306.

** Young, "Gathering," p. 306.

*** "Beneficial Effects of Polygamy: Remarks by President Brigham Young," *Journal of Discourses*, 11, 1866, pp. 266–72, here p. 269.

ancestors) was a polygamist. He appealed to several parabolic or poetic passages from the Bible to argue that Jesus was not only married, but took multiple wives. Pratt quoted John the Baptist, who said:"He that hath the bride is the bridegroom, but the friend of the bridegroom, which standeth and heareth him, rejoiceth greatly because of the bridegroom's voice" (John 3:39). Pratt also quoted Jesus in Mark 2:20, who said:"Can the children of the bridechamber mourn, as long as the bridegroom is with them? But the days will come, when the bridegroom shall be taken from them." As seen here, both biblical passages refer to Jesus as a "bridegroom."

Taken literally, these passages demonstrate that Jesus was married. In order to demonstrate that Jesus practiced plural marriage, Pratt appealed to the poem about a royal wedding in Psalm 45 (the king of this psalm is only vaguely described). Pratt argued that the royal figure of that psalm was Jesus. He concluded that "the great Messiah, who was the founder of the Christian religion, was a polygamist, as well as the Patriarch Jacob and the Prophet David, from whom he descended according to the flesh." Extending the logic of Brigham Young, Pratt argued that Jesus exemplified plural marriage. Indeed, Pratt wrote, "by marrying many honorable wives himself, [Jesus would] show all future generations that he approbated the plurality of Wives under the Christian dispensation, as well as under the dispensations in which His Polygamist ancestors lived."*

The crucial context to keep in mind is that the Mormons were a persecuted people in nineteenth-century America (most of America was a dangerous place for most non-Protestants). Their abnormal sexual ethic made them even more of a target. Given this external pressure, the leaders of the Mormon movement found it advantageous to justify their ethic by projecting it

---

* Pratt, O., "Celestial Marriage," in *The Seer*, vol.1.11 (1853), pp. 169–76, here p. 170.

back onto Jesus. Again, we witness Jesus being remade into the image of a specific culture.

Renan: Destroyer of Judaism (nineteenth century)

By the end of the nineteenth century – as compared with previous periods – biographies of Jesus were not difficult to find. The gospels attracted creative minds that focused on a selection of passages hoping to find a suggestion of Jesus's character and innermost thoughts. For example, Daniel Schenkel, writing in 1864, discovered a spiritually enlightened Jesus who saw clearly that the era of Jewish law would be over as soon as he was baptized. Schenkel's Jesus prepared the world for a new era, one without Jewish legalism and parochialism.

Schenkel was not alone: this portrait reflected the politics of Europe at the time. The historians of the nineteenth century were keenly interested in geniuses who burned down old eras with a spark of creativity. As Strauss said, Jesus was "the religious genius from whom a new epoch in the world's religious history proceeded."* Given the anti-Semitism running wild in Europe during this period, it is not surprising that the "old epoch" – the era that Jesus supposedly put away – was stereotypically Jewish.

French Catholic scholar, Ernest Renan (1823–92) is the biographer most overtly committed to this idea. Renan's Jesus was from Jewish parentage, but was able to cleanse himself of Judaism. So while he was born a Jew, Jesus left this identity behind to become the "destroyer of Judaism."*** In Renan's view, Jesus actu-

---

* Strauss, *Life of Jesus*, p. xxiv.
** Renan, E., *The Life of Jesus*, trans. C.E. Wilbour (London: Trübner & Co., Paternoster Row, 1864), p. 168.

ally became a member of the Aryan race. As such, he was able to establish a Christianity purified of Judaism. In probing into Jesus's (unwritten) thoughts, Renan found a mirror of his own anti-Semitism.

Figure 27 The Liesing altarpiece crucifix (circa 1980): Created by Austrian sculptor Alexander Silveri it is displayed at Liesing Parish Church, Vienna. It depicts Jesus in front of a cross, rather than hanging from it. Jesus's hands are extended in signs of blessing. His feet stand atop a globe with an engraved snake symbolizing Christ's victory over sin.

To fill out this context, Renan's published work also included political philosophy and theories of racial pseudoscience. He was convinced that the study of race would reveal the intrinsic characteristics of a people. Moreover, the Aryan race was, in his view, demonstrably superior to the Semitic race. As he projected these interests on the Gospel of John, Renan invented something of a proto-Nazi Christ.

Renan's Jesus foreshadows the ideology of Aryan superiority of the twentieth century. Prior to the Holocaust, many German theologians formed an institute with a single purpose: to create a new version of Christianity purified from Jewish influence. It was called the "Institute for the Study of Jewish Influence on the Life of the German Churches and the Removal of this Influence." In this context, Jesus was reborn as an Aryan.

Schweitzer: The miseducation of the Son of Man (twentieth century)

Albert Schweitzer (1875–1965) is perhaps best known for his medical work in Africa, for which he won a Nobel Peace Prize. Before that, however, his studies included theology and history. In 1906 Schweitzer wrote one of the most influential books about Jesus of the modern era. The English translation was *The Quest of the Historical Jesus: A Critical Study of its Progress from Reimarus to Wrede*.

Schweitzer's lasting contribution to Jesus studies is his emphasis on Jesus's status as an eschatological prophet. To an extent, H. S. Reimarus (in the eighteenth century) and William Wrede (in the nineteenth century) highlighted this aspect of Jesus before Schweitzer. But Schweitzer argued that this was the hinge upon which the entire project hung. Jesus's pronouncement that the "kingdom of God is at hand" encapsulated Jesus's belief that God would intervene in his lifetime to put an end to human history and establish a heavenly reign. In Schweitzer's opinion, previous biographies had underplayed Jesus's apocalyptic worldview, or had set it aside in favor of studying his ethics.

Schweitzer complained that nineteenth-century biographers had been preoccupied with Jesus's psychology. This, he thought, was an almost impossible task, and only invited a projection of the historian's own psychology. But for all of his complaining about biographers who guessed at Jesus's mind, Schweitzer himself could not avoid doing the same.

In his view, Jesus eventually lost his confidence that God would intervene to establish the kingdom. Looking to the prophet Isaiah (chapter 53), Jesus concluded that he must suffer and die. In doing so, Jesus hoped to force God's hand:

> [John the] Baptist appears and cries: "Repent, for the kingdom of heaven is at hand." Soon after that comes Jesus, and in the knowledge that He is the coming Son of Man lays hold of the wheel of the world to set it moving on that last revolution which is to bring all ordinary history to a close. It refuses to turn, and He throws Himself upon it. Then it does turn; and crushes Him. Instead of bringing in the eschatological conditions, He has destroyed them. The wheel rolls onward, and the mangled body of the one immeasurably great Man, who was strong enough to think of Himself as the spiritual ruler of mankind and to bend history to His purpose, is hanging upon it still. That is His victory and His reign.*

So Jesus was crucified but, again, was wrong. The world did not end. But in his death a new history had begun, one that Jesus did not envision. Schweitzer's historical Jesus is thus an alienating figure. Modern people will not be able to relate to him. His time, culture, and aspirations are simply too different for us to find common ground. "Jesus as a concrete historical personality

---

* Schweitzer, *Quest*, pp. 368–9.

remains a stranger to our time, but his spirit, which lies hidden in his words, is known in simplicity, and its influence is direct."*

Schweitzer's Jesus is a complex, ironic, and tragic figure. One is hard pressed to find a more fascinating portrait. But we must ask, was Jesus really preoccupied with old and new epochs? Or was this preoccupation a projection of Schweitzer's own prejudice?

Bultmann: Christian preaching must be translated (twentieth century)

After a century that produced creative biographies of Jesus, some scholars attempted to reclaim the Christ of Christian faith. In effect, these scholars retreated from historical reconstruction in pursuit of theology. German theologian, Martin Kähler (1835–1912) argued along these lines in his *The So-Called Historical Jesus and the Historic, Biblical Christ* (first published in 1896). Kähler argued that the gospels were theological documents and intended to be read as such. Those who tried to read them as historical documents, he argued, read them against the grain. In short, the "quest" for the historical Jesus was misguided. The Christian theologian, he argued, should focus on Jesus Christ as a figure who transcends his historical context. Kähler's Christ was therefore untethered from a first-century Jewish context. Incidentally, fewer biographies of Jesus were produced in Germany in the first half the twentieth century (as compared to the previous two centuries).

Kähler's student, Rudolf Bultmann (1884–1976) was among the exceptions. Bultmann intended to read Jesus's significance (like Kähler) theologically, but he was also interested in Jesus's historic, public career. Bultmann's *Jesus* was published in 1926 and

---

* Schweitzer, *Quest*, p. 400.

placed Jesus firmly within the context of first-century Jewish life. Bultmann did not intend to write a psychological biography. He believed that this approach had met a dead end. He did, however, sketch the basic elements of Jesus's life and teachings. Bultmann thought that Jesus was an interesting historical topic; but he, like Kähler, believed that the historical Jesus was only a precursor to theology, and not ultimately important for the Christian. Bultmann believed that the Christ of personal encounter was far more important than the historical Jesus. It was Bultmann's theological writings – those focused on the beliefs and formation of early Christianity – that created a lasting impact. Indeed it is difficult to overstate Bultmann's influence on this field of research.

In many ways, his passion to reconstruct Jesus had been overshadowed by a passion to reconstruct the early Church. Bultmann was a prominent figure of a theory called "Form Criticism." He and his students became famous for a method of classifying the various units of gospel tradition based on their literary forms. Each passage within the gospels was seen as a literary unit. Importantly, each saying and story revealed something about the social setting of the first Christians and revealed very little about the historical Jesus. Moreover, the Form Critics created the early Christians in their own image, so to speak. It almost became a mantra among these literary-oriented scholars to say that the first Christians were all but uninterested in Jesus as a historical figure. Those first Christians encountered Jesus as a spiritual and religious experience. As such, the Jesus that really mattered – both in the first and the twentieth centuries – was a Jesus that transcended historical context.

So great was Bultmann's impact that we might be better off to think of his career in two facets. There is Bultmann "the theologian" and Bultmann "the historian." Admittedly, the first overshadowed the second. Bultmann "the theologian" wanted to make the gospel intelligible for the modern mind. He argued that the themes and message of the New Testament were conveyed in the "language of mythology." He continues: "To this extent [early Christian preaching about Jesus] is incredible to modern man, for he is convinced that the mythical view of the world is obsolete."* The modern mind, according to Bultmann, cannot be expected to think in mythological categories. So Bultmann attempted to translate the "essential" elements in the New Testament for the modern world. In order for Jesus to be encountered by the modern mind, the "mythical framework" of the preaching about Jesus must be "stripped." He writes:

> We are therefore bound to ask whether, when we preach the Gospel to-day, we expect our converts to accept not only the Gospel message, but also the mythical view of the world in which it is set. If not, does the New Testament embody a truth which is quite independent of its mythical settings? If it does, theology must undertake the task of stripping [preaching about Jesus] from its mythical framework, of "demythologizing" it.**

For Bultmann, the "mythical frameworks" of the gospels hid the essential Christian message. The mindset that worked for an ancient worldview now blocked Jesus from a modern worldview. You might say that Bultmann "the theologian" was an evangelist to the children of the Enlightenment.

Bultmann "the historian" worked from the same premise, but had a different agenda. He believed that the language of mythology also hid most of Jesus's life from historical research. So, in addition to stripping away mythology from Christian preaching, Bultmann also stripped Christian preaching from the authentic Jesus. The former he did in service to modern theology; the latter in service to modern history. We might visualize these two agendas like this:

---

* Bultmann, R., "The New Testament and Mythology," in *Kerygma and Myth: A Theological Debate*, ed. H.-W. Bartsch (New York: Harper and Row, 1953), pp. 2–3
** Bultmann, "Mythology," p. 3.

For the theologian (agenda one): mythology hides authentic Christian preaching. So strip away the language of myth and recover the essence of the faith.

For the historian (agenda two): mythology hides the historical Jesus. So strip away the language of myth and recover the authentic Jesus.

Bultmann all but disassociated his historical interests in Jesus from his theological interests in Christian preaching. As such, we see Bultmann turn the agenda of Jefferson on its head. While both men attempted to divorce Jesus from the mythological stories about him, they had different ideas about the next step. Jefferson thought that Jesus's authentic ethical teachings should become the foundation of modern religion. Bultmann thought that modern religion should be built on the essence of the first Christian preachers.

Linnemann: Bultmannian backlash (twentieth century)

Bultmann's impact on students of the gospels, Christian origins, and the historical Jesus was enormous, and continues to be felt today. For much of the twentieth century, scholars endeavored to stratify the layers of the gospels to discover what was original to Jesus, what was part of the earliest Christian preaching, or what was invented much later. The project was called "Form Criticism" and promised to apply a more scientific system of classification for the traditions of Jesus and the gospels. For generations, historical–critical scholars were either motivated by Form Criticism or set against it in reaction to its success.

In some ways, Bultmann was a victim of his own success. Two related consequences of his project unfolded. First, Form Criticism became preoccupied with the social settings of the Church. Almost every word attributed to Jesus was thought to reveal something about a hypothetical community. For example, the Gospel of John was thought to have come from John's community. In this view, each gospel was composed within a group setting and betrayed the concerns of the group. Moreover, these communities were thought to be highly creative; they invented a mythology of Jesus based on their own religious experiences and social concerns. Rather than reconstructing a historical figure, these scholars began to reconstruct the imaginations of hypothetical groups. Second, rather than making the "essence" of Jesus more attractive to modern folk, Bultmann became a villain to many Christians. His theories were so compelling that many people of faith had a visceral reaction to him. Some among the hyperconservative rejected historical study altogether. This was the case with one of his own students: Eta Linnemann (1926–2009).

MEET THIS WORD: POSTMODERN

Postmodern entered into English usage in the twentieth century. The term sometimes refers to a thing, idea, style, etc., that post-dates the modern version of that thing, idea, style, etc. Postmodern also refers to a philosophical method of critique that questions (or deconstructs) the assumptions and results of modern thought.

Eta Linnemann's early work on the parables and passion of Jesus was much in line with her mentor's project. She set out to explain the social settings that gave rise to the stories. The sayings of Jesus (for the most part) were composed by and for the early Christians. Supernatural accounts within the gospels were wholesale invention. Linnemann did well in academia. Her books were widely read and she took a professorship at Philipps University in Marburg, Germany. Indeed, she felt that her research was a service to God. But Linnemann had a crisis of conscience: after years of historical training and form-critical research, she concluded that no meaningful truth could come from her professional life.

Worse, her research had created an obstacle to Christian preaching. She published the following reflection in 1985:

> Today I know that I owe those initial insights to the beginning effects of God's grace. At first, however, what I realized led me into profound disillusionment. I reacted by drifting toward addictions which might dull my misery. I became enslaved to watching television and fell into an increasing state of alcohol dependence. My bitter personal experience finally convinced me of the truth of the Bible's assertion: "Whoever finds his life will lose it" (Matt. 10:39). At that point God led me to vibrant Christians who knew Jesus personally as their Lord and Savior. I heard their testimonies as they reported what God had done in their lives. Finally God himself spoke to my heart by means of a Christian brother's words. By God's grace and love I entrusted my life to Jesus.*

By her own words, Linnemann had "turned Evangelical." By entrusting her life to Jesus, she was pulled from depression, idleness, and alcoholism. By any measure, her conversion transformed her with highly positive results. She, however, adopted an adversarial relationship with her past, including her previous relationship with Jesus.

Linnemann's spiritual encounter with Jesus, as she saw it, forced her to recant and repent from her former profession. She declared her historical study to be sinful and derided her former publications: "I regard everything that I taught and wrote before I entrusted my life to Jesus as refuse."** She threw her books and articles away, and invited her readers to do the same. Her new existential relationship with Jesus convinced her to throw away her previous portrait.

---

* Linnemann, E., *Historical Criticism of the Bible: Methodology or Ideology: Reflections of a Bultmannian Turned Evangelical*, trans. Robert W. Yarbrough (Grand Rapids: Kregel, 1990), p. 18.
** Linnemann, *Historical Criticism*, p. 20.

In my judgment, Linnemann's experience echoes many students and seminarians who encounter historical Jesus research. It is common for these students to either embrace historical study (as Linnemann did in her early life), or choose an almost anti-intellectual path whereby faith and history compete (as she did in her later life). But it must be said that Linnemann's particular reaction to her former life would not have been possible without a keen intellectual capacity to critique her own method. Her post-conversion publications take a bitter and hostile tone against university culture and historical-critical study in general.

While her tone and rhetoric are extreme, Linnemann made an astute and necessary observation: the historian can only ever disguise her/his ideology with a veneer of objectivity. She argued that historical-critical study is not a method – it is an ideology rife with prejudice. Certainly she offers us a partial explanation for why historians continue to project their own biases and ideals onto Jesus.

While it would be misleading to label her as "postmodern," Linnemann teaches us one of the most important lessons of the postmodern critique: scientific study tends to break down what it observes. The modern tendency is to parse, reduce, classify, and utilize. But what happens when the modern, critical eye turns on itself? What happens when the intellectual mind begins to parse, reduce, classify, and utilize itself? The inevitable result is that we begin to critique the criticism.

Gutiérrez: Jesus as a model for liberation (twentieth and twenty-first centuries)

Gustavo Gutiérrez (1928–) is best known for his theological impact; he is celebrated as the father of "liberation theology." A Dominican priest from Peru, he has dedicated much of his life to the people of Lima and the study of global poverty. His practical and theoretical focus on poverty colored his interpretation of Jesus's life. It is equally true that his devotion to Jesus colored his interest in poverty. Gutiérrez studied medicine, psychology, and philosophy before becoming a professional theologian.

In his book, *A Theology of Liberation: History, Politics, Salvation* (1971), Gutiérrez describes three kinds of poverty: material poverty (privation); spiritual poverty (openness and trust in a loving God); and voluntary poverty (protest against systems that enforce material poverty). The last of these, voluntary poverty, is based on an interpretation of the doctrine of Christ's incarnation. Gutiérrez argues that Christ chose to live alongside impoverished people in order to love the poor and to challenge the oppressive systems causing them to suffer. Followers of Christ (of all times and places) are therefore commended to embrace a life of "spiritual childhood" by renouncing material wealth.

In service to this program, Gutiérrez situates a reconstruction of Jesus's life and ministry. He begins by drawing several parallels between Jesus and the so-called Zealots. Gutiérrez supposed that Jesus and his followers had a great deal in common with the political revolutionaries of his day.* He was compelled by the many similarities between Jesus and these zealous ideologues. The key difference, according to Gutiérrez, was that Jesus was not invested in nationalism. Jesus's message, rather, was universal in scope.

Gutiérrez's Jesus does not fit well into the other major Jewish groups. Jesus rejected the power of the elite Sadducees. Jesus rejected the oppressive policies of Herod. Jesus criticized

---

* The consensus among contemporary scholars is that the Zealots did not coalesce as a political movement until the end of the first century. Gutiérrez therefore uses this category anachronistically. But there were certainly political revolutionaries (or those who held seditious views) during Jesus's time.

the "religion made up of purely external laws and obser-
vances," which brought him "into a violent confrontation with
the Pharisees."* Finally, Gutiérrez sets Jesus against the Roman
authorities. Jesus, while not a Zealot, was considered a Zealot
by Rome and executed as such. "Jesus died at the hands of the
political authorities, the oppressors of the Jewish people."*** Jesus,
in this program, was an ally to the Jewish common folk, but an
opponent to all who oppressed them. Finally, Jesus's resurrection
proclaims both spiritual and political liberation.

Gutiérrez's Jesus is clearly a historical reconstruction meant
to challenge what he saw as a hierarchical and over-spiritual-
ized Christianity. In his view, far too many Christians "take it
for granted that Jesus was not interested in political life: his mission was purely religious."**** But this assumption, he claims, fails
to recognize Jesus's historical personality. "The life of Jesus is
thus placed outside history, unrelated to the real forces at play.
Jesus and those whom he befriended, or whom he confronted
and whose hostility he earned, are deprived of all human con-
tent." Gutiérrez argues that we must reconsider Jesus's life "with
respect for the historical Jesus, not forcing the facts in terms of

---

* Gutiérrez, G., *A Theology of Liberation*, 15th Anniversary Edition
with a New Introduction by the Author (New York: Maryknoll, 2000),
p. 132. It is disappointing that Gutiérrez chooses to repeat the common Christian falsehood that the religion of the Pharisees was legalistic
and oppressive. Moreover, theologies that set Jesus against his kinsmen
contribute to the historic Christian tendency to persecute Jews. While
Gutiérrez should be applauded for emphasizing Jesus's teachings about
poverty, he undermines his own program by echoing a theological assumption that promotes a centuries-old form of oppression. The fact
that he uses the word "violent confrontation" (even if metaphorical) in
this context is even more troubling.
** Gutiérrez, *A Theology of Liberation*, pp. 132–3.
*** Gutiérrez, *A Theology of Liberation*, p. 130.

our current concerns."* Gutiérrez argued that Jesus's life, once contextualized properly within his historical setting, would bring about a better, more relevant Christian theology. He called this a "theology of liberation."

Liberation theology now takes several different forms. Gutiérrez's program, while imperfect, influenced the work of James Hal Cone. Cone built upon this foundation to create a systematic theology conversant with the African-American experience, while Andrew Park extended this work in conversation with the Korean experience. The theology of Gutiérrez is often echoed in the words and actions of Pope Francis.

Future prospects: Four inspiring voices (twenty-first century)

From the 1970s onward (reaching a climax in the 1990s), books about the historical Jesus became an industry. Scholars like John Dominic Crossan and N. Thomas Wright sold millions of books and were invited to speak globally on the topic of Jesus. Jesus was the star of films, documentaries, and countless magazine covers. To ride the media momentum generated by popular culture, seminary and university professors were interviewed by major news outlets to affirm or correct the latest revisionist history of Jesus's life. The following four names, have not (yet) received the most screen time or trending buzz on Twitter, but their advances in historical Jesus research continue to inspire my work. They, to my mind, point the way to future innovation and correction within the field: Dale C. Allison, Jr.; Chris Keith; Amy-Jill Levine; and Dagmar Winter.

These four are not the Mount Rushmore of Jesus research, commemorating past greats. They are not The Beatles,

---

* Gutiérrez, *A Theology of Liberation*, pp. 131–2.

representing generational popularity. Allison, Keith, Levine, and Winter are more like the Four Horsemen of the Apocalypse, portending the near future.* I will not attempt to encapsulate the body of their respective works, which is considerable. These few paragraphs will only touch on what I have found to be their most compelling impact on the field at large.

Amy-Jill Levine has done much to correct misconceptions of first-century Jewish life and its relationship with Jesus's emerging legacy in Christian thought. This feature of her work extends the works of David Flusser, E. P. Sanders and others. Put simply: *How can we understand Jesus and his significance if we misunderstand his culture?* Understanding first-century Jewish life requires nuance and an appreciation of complexity. Correcting longstanding and simplistic assumptions helps us better understand Jesus and Christian origins. Levine is also candid about her investment in continued Jewish and Christian well-being. Approaching Jesus from a Jewish perspective, her work educates both Jews and Christians by making sense of Jesus as a rabbi in the first century. Given the backdrop of Ignatius, Marcion, the Gospel of Gamaliel, Renan (discussed in this book), and so many other episodes of anti-Judaism in Christian history, a continued interest in Jesus's Jewishness is good medicine.

Dale Allison has brought the highest level of sophistication to Jesus's prophetic voice with an eye to his apocalyptic and eschatological aims. In this way, he builds from the theories of Albert Schweitzer and others who emphasized Jesus's end-of-the-age approach and divine judgment worldview. Often he's argued this over and against those who would paint Jesus only as a sage or social reformer. But what I find most interesting in Allison's work is borne from his growing skepticism of the gospels as historical narratives. He does not read the gospels as fiction, but even if these

---

* Horse people? Horse attendants? Horse administrators? Equestrians? Gauchos? Buckaroos?

early stories derive from memory, memory can be frail and often misleading. While I do not share Allison's point of departure (i.e. I am more optimistic), I am compelled by the method that came from it.* Allison argues that if we want to see the historical Jesus, we must find emphases, themes, and repetitions that are scattered in multiple documents and genres. To use the analogy of visual art, the historian must step back and survey the repeated features of a series of portraits along a similar theme. For this reason, I've called Allison's method "Historical Impressionism."

Dagmar Winter (alongside her mentor Gerd Theissen) put forth one of the most important innovations in the field. Although she has received too little attention for it, her work on "plausible" historical effects calls centuries of historical Jesus research into question. She suggests that the obvious contradictions in the gospels offer our best hope for a plausible historical portrait. In other words, contradictions are not obstacles to historical reconstruction; in fact, quite the contrary. Previous generations of scholarship would discover a contradiction in the gospels and reject the offending claims (as dubious and therefore without historical value). For example, if John 3:22 claims that Jesus conducted baptisms, but John 4:2 claims otherwise, most scholars would note the contradiction and look elsewhere for more solid historical data.** In other words, because of this

---

* It should be noted that Allison's skepticism is not thoroughgoing. He seems quite confident about the historian's ability to reconstruct the general impression left by Jesus. While he is skeptical of the particular details in the Gospels, Allison (at times) seems confident about his overall reconstruction.

** John 3:22 reads: "After this Jesus and his disciples went into the Judean countryside, and he spent some time there with them and baptized." Here we have a clear indication that Jesus, alongside his disciples, baptized people. But the narrator of John is uncomfortable with this claim. So he inserts a parenthetical statement in John 4:1–3: "Now when

contradiction, we can never know whether Jesus himself baptized his followers. But Winter argues that if the contradiction can be explained by a common solution, we are very close to historical truth. The truth is what best explains both sides of the contradiction. These "accidental" incongruities offer our best hope to arrive at a plausible portrait. It is not the historian's task to nail down the actual past, but to explain a plausible history of effects. So sometimes contradictory historical claims lead us to a solution that explains both. If a good explanation for both claims can be argued convincingly, we can arrive at a plausible fact about Jesus.

Chris Keith's primary expertise is the study of literacy and the use of texts in first-century Jewish life and early Christianity. He has also emerged as the leading voice of social memory theory in historical Jesus research. Keith builds from the work of Jens Schröter, Tom Thatcher, Alan Kirk, and others.* He is not the first to apply social memory to Jesus research, but no person has

---

Jesus learned that the Pharisees had heard, 'Jesus is making and baptizing more disciples than John' (although it was not Jesus himself but his disciples who baptized) he left Judea and started back to Galilee."

Sometimes the narrator of John's Gospel will insert a parenthetical statement that contradicts the natural flow of the story. So the historian asks, why is the narrator so concerned that we might think that Jesus was baptizing? And why is it a problem that the Pharisees think that Jesus was baptizing?

Almost every commentary on John tells us that the narrator (1) wants to elevate Jesus at the Baptist's expense, and (2) is out to make the Judean leadership look bad. I don't doubt that both of these agendas have colored the story in John 4:1–3. But embedded in this politicized counter-memory is a memory of a specific rumor about Jesus. Could it be that some Pharisees in the late first century believed that Jesus baptized people *en masse*? Given the way the narrator presents this datum, I would tend to think so.

* I happily and gratefully count myself among these "others."

published more on the topic. Social memory theory holds that no kind of memory is entirely "private" or "individual" because all memory is framed within social interaction. Even our private thoughts are motivated and confined by our socially conditioned minds. Additionally, memory is fluid. It is always evolving to meet the needs of the present. This is true of both individuals and groups. By applying these insights to Jesus, Keith reads the gospels as sites of collective memory. The best way to reconstruct Jesus, Keith argues, is to account for the gospels in the forms that they are presented. It is the historian's task to explain how early Christians came to think what they did, and this means explaining both their accuracies and inaccuracies to the extent that it is possible. He rejects previous attempts to divide the gospels into smaller units and label them as either "authentic" or "inauthentic." Rather, every bit of the gospels must be evaluated as social memory (which both distorts and continues the impact of past events). Jesus can be reconstructed, therefore, by analyzing the ways that he was remembered.

Conclusion

For most of the two-thousand year history of Jesus portraiture, creative thinkers have been preoccupied with how Jesus fits within theology. Those who were not interested in "God-talk" tended to use Jesus to portray something about the human experience. In a conscious departure from these pursuits, modern intelligentsia tried to correct "uncritical" portraits of Jesus's life. To this end, professional historians attempted to better their understanding of his cultural matrix, and drew connections between Jesus's teachings and his political climate. For many, Jesus was a force of personality who launched a new age. As such, Jesus's legacy was used to explain the rise of a new religion.

In the modern era, Jesus's Jewishness became a defining issue for explaining his life and teaching. Whereas previous generations cast Jesus as an archetype for humanity or a heavenly agent, recent historians put a spotlight on Jesus's ancient and particular context. In many versions of anti-Jewish intelligentsia throughout the centuries, Jesus's Jewishness was questionable (or rejected outright), but his life in the culture and worship of Jewish Galilee is now assumed by the discipline.

But historians are not immune to the problems of bias. Modern historians, while perhaps more critical than their predecessors, continue to repeat old assumptions and introduce new errors. This is why the "historical Jesus" is an ongoing discussion, rather than a definitive solution.

Five books about philosophy and method in Jesus research

Allison, D.C., Jr. *Constructing Jesus: Memory, Imagination, and History.* (Grand Rapids: Baker Academic, 2013).

Denton, D.L. Jr. *Historiography and Hermeneutics in Jesus Studies: An Examination of the Work of John Dominic Crossan and Ben F. Meyer.* (The Library of New Testament Studies; London: Bloomsbury/ T&T Clark, 2004).

Le Donne, A. *The Historiographical Jesus: Memory, Typology, and the Son of David.* (Waco: Baylor University Press, 2009).

Meyer, B.F. *Critical Realism and the New Testament.* (Princeton Theological Monograph Series; Eugene: Pickwick, 1989).

Theissen G. and Winter, D. *The Quest for the Plausible Jesus: The Question of Criteria*, trans. M.E. Boring. (Louisville: Westminster/John Knox Press, 2002).

5

Jesus in pop culture

"I have been so great in boxing they had to create an image like Rocky, a white image on the screen, to counteract my image in the ring. America has to have its white images, no matter where it gets them. Jesus, Wonder Woman, Tarzan and Rocky."

Muhammad Ali

Introduction: Relations and reflections

Jesus plays an important element in the history of book culture, but not necessarily academic books. In fact, early book culture might give us a window into common, day-to-day conversations.

The early Christians were among the first (perhaps the very first) to adopt the codex rather than the scroll for their sacred texts. The word Bible comes from the Latin and Greek words for "book." The printing of the Gutenberg Bible marked the beginning of mass production of books in the West. While it is true that Jesus has been an important topic for the intelligentsia, Jesus has had a much larger impact on pop culture.

For example, in the fifteenth century Thomas à Kempis (himself well educated) wrote a book to teach spiritual practice to commoners. It was titled *The Imitation of Christ* (circa 1420) and it became one of the most popular books ever produced. The book shows little interest in Jesus as a figure in history. Rather, it teaches Christians how to be devoted to Jesus and to imitate his life in discipline and humility. *The Imitation of Christ* remains one of the most widely used devotional guides among Christians. More importantly, some of its key insights are passed from preacher to Christian, from Sunday school teacher to student, and from spiritual guide to seeker without explicit reference to the book. In short, some of the ideas of Thomas à Kempis are so entrenched in Christian spiritual teaching that people echoing him do not know it. Such is the case with pop culture: a point of "common knowledge" may relate to book culture, but it takes on a life of its own.

It is therefore difficult to measure Jesus's popularity in the modern world by surveying intellectual thought, but popular references to Jesus in books of all kinds (not limited to academia) might give us some insight. Using Google Books Ngram Viewer, one can survey a large selection of books that have been digitized. The Ngram Viewer shows how many times a word or phrase has been used in publications over a period of time. Consider the following chart (Figure 28) that surveys English-language books from 1800. Here we can see the popular usage of the names Jesus Christ, Abraham Lincoln, and Adolf Hitler.*

Notice that the combination of the two words "Jesus" and "Christ" declines in popular use from the mid-nineteenth century to the twentieth century. This decline suggests that the English-speaking world had become less interested in the name Jesus Christ. Nonetheless, even at the lowest point of this trend (circa 1940) the name Jesus Christ was still twice as popular in

---

* A survey of phrases used in the Google Books selection can only reveal so much. This chart (albeit imprecise) does probably indicate general trends of popular thought. In this specific search, I used the fields "Jesus Christ, Abraham Lincoln, Adolf Hitler."

Figure 28 Ngram of Christ, Lincoln, and Hitler
X-axis represents the time period of the publications surveyed; Y-axis represents the percentage of usage of the names within these publications.

usage as Adolf Hitler or Abraham Lincoln. (I've selected these two names to represent historical figures who continue to attract attention in pop culture.) The question, then, is not *whether* Jesus is a pop-culture topic, but *how is Jesus used* as a pop-culture topic?

The following chart shows a dramatic increase in the phrase "relationship with Jesus" from 1970 to 2005. It also shows that before the twentieth century, the phrase was not popular.

The notion that the Christian believer can have a personal relationship with Jesus is not new. For example, Augustine's

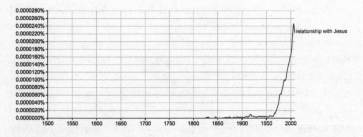

Figure 29 Ngram of "relationship with Jesus"
X-axis represents the time period of the publications surveyed; Y-axis represents the percentage of usage of the phrase within these publications.

treatment of the Trinity in the fifth century explained how the believer can relate to the relational God. Thomas à Kempis portrays Jesus relating to his followers in dialogue in the 1400s. So the trend we see post-1970 is not the invention of a new idea; rather, it represents a new emphasis. From 1970 to 2005 – especially among evangelical Christians – it was increasingly common to describe one's devotion to Jesus as having a personal relationship with him. This same period saw an increase in the phrase "born again Christian." It is not surprising, then, that these phrases were viewed in both positive and negative ways. Those who self-identified as "born again," or as having a "relationship with Jesus," viewed these popular phrases in almost entirely positive terms.

Conversely, in the English-speaking world (and elsewhere) this period saw a popular backlash against religion in general, and against Christianity specifically. While still a relative minority, those outside academia were more willing to voice their disillusionment with Christianity and Jesus devotion in the late twentieth century. While the popular use of Jesus's name remained high, we should not assume that Jesus was popular with every writer using his name.

So, in addition to the expected mirror effect (i.e. Jesus reflects the assumptions and ideals of the culture), portraits of Jesus in pop culture also take on a subversive effect. When artistic and political voices want to criticize Christianity, Jesus becomes a tool to do so. Either (a) Jesus is painted as someone with opposite ideals than the typical, modern Christian, or (b) Jesus is painted in a negative light.

Another word on the "mirror effect" is warranted: portraits of Jesus reflect the culture of the artist. This much is obvious. But given that Jesus reflects both the devotional needs of religious culture and the critical needs of secular culture, his popular portraits invariably contrast and compete. Jesus's face and teaching, therefore, has been co-opted for and against religious institutions.

Clephane: The cross from below

Hymns are an integral part of the Christian encounter with Jesus, and hymn singing was a feature of the first house churches in the first-century Mediterranean. While many hymns come from famous Christian leaders like Martin Luther (1483–1546) and Charles Wesley (1707–88), some began as expressions of faith and prayers by common folk. In such cases, hymns can serve as windows into religious encounters of Jesus outside the clerical class. Hymns are not now, perhaps, important parts of contemporary pop culture. But for centuries, spiritual songs preserved the souls of common folk and projected their faith and aspirations into future generations. The story of Elizabeth Clephane projects a voice that would not have been heard if not for the newspaper that published her words after her death. Being of little means, geographically remote, and female, her voice had no microphone.

Elizabeth Cecilia Douglas Clephane (1830–69) was a Christian living in Scotland without wealth or fame. She was known, however, among her Melrose neighbors for bringing relief to the poor and sick. Clephane was reputed to have sold her horse and carriage to provide for the disadvantaged. Before her death (just short of her fortieth year) she wrote at least two hymns. These were published posthumously.*

One of her hymns was titled "Beneath the Cross of Jesus" and tells the story of the wearisome journey of a spiritual pilgrim. Troubled by the "burning of the noontide heat" the pilgrim takes comfort in the shade cast by Jesus's cross. She writes:

---

* Hawn, C.M., *History of Hymns: "Beneath the Cross of Jesus."* [Online]. (URL https://www.umcdiscipleship.org/resources/history-of-hymns-beneath-the-cross-of-jesus). (Accessed March 29, 2018).

Upon that cross of Jesus
Mine eye at times can see
The very dying form of One,
Who suffered there for me;
And from my smitten heart, with tears,
Two wonders I confess,
The wonders of His glorious love,
And my own worthlessness.

This stanza illustrates the common notion of salvation associated with Jesus's cross. What was once a symbol of terror and shame evolved in the Christian imagination into a source of comfort. Clephane also echoes the longstanding Christian belief that Jesus's undeserved suffering alleviates the suffering that Christians might experience without Jesus's sacrifice. In brief, Christians most often believe that human sin brings suffering, but that Jesus's cross solves the problem of sin. This is understood to be the ultimate expression of divine love.

Finally, Clephane's hymn expresses a sense of "worthlessness." This is expressed in comparison. Jesus's act of sacrificial love and great suffering seems such an extravagant display that no believer is worthy of it. While the final line might suggest low self-esteem, it is meant to express a "smitten heart" and a sense of "glorious love." The cross in this hymn is a stand in for Jesus as savior and lover.

Jesus – husband and lover

One of the most common notions about Jesus in pop culture is the assumption that he associated with prostitutes. I will confess that I repeated this trope in one of my books. I wrote:

The canonical gospels betray [Jesus's] reputation for being a partying hedonist and his often socially inappropriate associations with women. Jesus seems to have kept regular company with hookers and vamps.*

While Jesus does seem to have a hedonistic reputation in the gospels, I was wrong to say that he kept regular company with hookers. If I had done better research, I would have learned that Jesus never associates with prostitutes in the gospels. In fact, Jesus does not associate with prostitutes in any first-century narrative. So how and when did this rumor about Jesus start?

In short, although there is no explicit claim of this in the gospels, it has often been assumed that Mary Magdalene was a prostitute. This claim, it turns out, is a medieval fiction. Pope Gregory I (591 CE) assumed as much in a sermon, and the oft-repeated rumor has become "common knowledge" ever since. In 1260, an archbishop named Jacobus de Voragine wrote a story about Mary Magdalene telling how she fell into prostitution. This assumption about Mary was retold in Nikos Kazantzakis's novel, *The Last Temptation of Christ*, in 1955, and Martin Scorsese turned the novel into a film in 1988. In the popular imagination of the Christianized West, Mary Magdalene had become a prostitute. There was, therefore, little reason to question Jesus's public association with prostitutes.

Spinning the error ahead further, Jesus's sexuality found a new spotlight in the twentieth century. *The Last Temptation of Christ* told a story of Jesus's imaginary hope for a life of normalcy (including sexuality). Some Christians boycotted the film and attempted to ban the book because the thought of Jesus's sexual imagination was sacrilegious. Because Jesus's sexuality became a hot topic, and because Mary's legacy had been sexualized, it was only natural to create a match. Jesus had been reinvented as Mary's boyfriend.

---

* Le Donne, A., *Historical Jesus: What can we know and how can we know it?* (Grand Rapids: Eerdmans, 2010), p. 44.

It wasn't until Dan Brown's massively popular novel, *The Da Vinci Code*, that the general public began to imagine a Mary devoid of prostitution. The idea that she was Jesus's lover was fascinating; but the proposal that she was his wife was a bestseller. In Brown's detective mystery, a modern Frenchwoman, Sophie, learns of an ancient cover-up concerning the marriage of Jesus and Mary. According to the story, this secret "history" has been communicated through the work of Renaissance artist Leonardo Da Vinci. Brown depicts a conversation between Sophie and a historian as both are looking at Da Vinci's *Last Supper*.

> "That, my dear," Teabing replied, "is Mary Magdalene."
> Sophie turned. "The prostitute?"
> Teabing drew a short breath, as if the word had injured him person-ally. "Magdalene was no such thing. That unfortunate misconception is the legacy of a smear campaign launched by the early Church."*

This portrait of Magdalene as the secret wife of Jesus was too com-pelling to ignore, and just scandalous enough to turn a fun detective novel into an international debate. The novel dominated the *New York Times* bestsellers list for over two years (2003–5) and was boy-cotted by many churches when it was made into a film. Multiple books by Christian scholars and apologists were published for the sole purpose of exposing the historical inaccuracies of the book.

But for all of the book's fictive elements, Dan Brown prob-ably did the most to expose Pope Gregory's fallacy to the general public. The fictitious Mary of *The Da Vinci Code* was not a pros-titute. Brown's Mary was, however, royalty. A key element to the plot line was that both Mary and Jesus were of royal lineage. This draws its inspiration, in part, from Archbishop Jacobus's historical fiction in the thirteenth century. Brown discarded what he did

---

* Brown, D., *The Da Vinci Code* (reprint from 2003; New York: An-chor, 2009), pp. 319–20.

not like of the medieval fiction and kept what would most help his plot. Ironically, while his fiction successfully undermined the erroneous image of Mary as a prostitute, it capitalized on Jesus's sexual normalcy. In this way, it tapped the same cultural nerve *The Last Temptation of Christ* had.

Jesus, black and white

When the emerging study of race began in post-Enlightenment Europe, the idea went hand in hand with racial hierarchy (what we now call racism). Those inventing the concept thought that they would find that science backed up their prejudices. Their prejudices included the notions that intelligence and moral inclination could be predicted by racial heritage. So before the concept of "whiteness" existed, the framework for modern racism was shaped by the ideal of Eurocentric normalcy. European physical features (phenotypes) were ideal; other variations of physicality were less than ideal.

MEET THIS WORD: ETHNICITY

Ethnicity is a word coined in 1953 that borrowed from the Greek word *ethnos*, meaning "people/nation." The word, as it was conceived within anthropology, was invented in counter-distinction to race. Because the concept of race was thought to carry negative connotations of racism, a new label was required. The consensus among ethnologists is that ethnicity is not a genetic category. Rather, as one introductory textbook defines it, an ethnicity is a people with varying combinations of (1) a common proper name; (2) a myth of common ancestry; (3) shared commemoration; (4) one or more elements of common culture; (5) a link with a (physical or symbolic) homeland; (6) a sense of solidarity with a homeland.

---

* Hutchinson, J. and Smith, A.D., "Introduction," in *Ethnicity*, ed. J. Hutchinson and A.D. Smith (Oxford: Oxford University Press, 1996), pp. 6–7.

The portraiture of Jesus during this period is undoubtedly
... this ideolog... In order to appreciate the complexity of
...made clear. First, many of the
...body types) painted
...traits of Jesus influ-
...m, the assumption of
...ial ideals. Second, the
...unked on sociological
...(primarily "black" and
...ur own making. Indeed
...ep-seated and widespread
...d West with an almost per-
...ess of Jesus – who embod-
...r collective consciousness.
...created a vicious cycle:
...e our racial ideals; our racial
... So to our eyes, the iconic
...recognizably Jesus – is white.
...tered pop culture, civil rights
activist, Mal... ...e iconic portrait of a white
Jesus. He forcefully argued that the black American Christian had
been brainwashed:

> He's not interested in any religion of his own. He believes in a white
> Jesus, white Mary, white angels, and he's trying to get to a white
> heaven. When you listen to him in his church singing, he sings a
> song, I think they call it, "Wash me white as snow." He wants to be
> – he wants to be turned white so he can go to heaven with a white
> man. It's not his fault; it's actually not his fault. But this is the state
> of his mind. This is the result of 400 years of brainwashing here in
> America.*

---

* Quoted from "The Race Problem," January 23, 1963. (URL http://
ccnmtl.columbia.edu/projects/mmt/mxp/speeches/mxt15.html). (Accessed March 29, 2018).

While responses to Malcolm X's critique varied, it was taken to heart by a few prominent Christian theologians. Most notably, theologian James Hal Cone was influenced by this critique. Remaining within the Christian tradition, Cone began to exorcise white supremacy from his Christianity. Importantly, to follow Jesus was to identify with the socially dispossessed – after all, Jesus identified with the poor and the outcasts of his day. "Through God's love, the black man is given the power to *become*, the power to make others recognize him."* Notably, according to Cone, such divine empowerment was possible only if the black Christian remained black.

Still, the portrait of a white Jesus continues to dominate the Christianized West. So entrenched is the image of a white Jesus in our collective consciousness that the topic is usually only addressed in pop culture when an artist deviates from it. And typically, it isn't until we see the portrait of a black Jesus that we discuss our standard assumptions of his ethnicity. In their 2012 publication, *The Color of Christ*, Blum and Harvey explain how the problem plays out in pop culture:

> The long history of Jesus and race left sacred whiteness challenge-able and even changeable. But for the most part it was still assumable and marketable. As part of the *Da Vinci Code* craze, millions of readers stared intently at European artwork to see if Mary Magdalene was really at the Last Supper with the white Jesus… The paintings supposedly held secrets of sexual power, [novelist, Dan] Brown fantasized, but no one wondered about the racial hierarchy hidden in plain sight. Dan Brown never wondered if the whiteness of the painted figures had any meaning at all. Only a few years earlier, hundreds of millions sat spellbound as they watched a white, brown-eyed Jesus (even though the actor portraying him had blue eyes) beaten to a bloody pulp. No one in Mel Gibson's *The Passion of the Christ*

---

* Cone, J.H., *Black Theology and Black Power* (2nd edn; San Francisco: HarperSanFrancisco, 1989 [1969]), p. 52.

(2004) spoke English, but it did not matter. Watching Jesus and his body mattered.*

It is now not difficult to find artistic expressions of Jesus depicted with various ethnic phenotypes. A quick image search online for "ethnic Jesus" will yield several variations. But this fact only reinforces the default of Jesus's whiteness in pop culture. Jesus is almost exclusively white if the image search is reduced simply to one word: "Jesus."

As should be expected with pop culture controversies, the standard depiction of a white Jesus draws a small, but vociferous, backlash. The Urban Dictionary (usually devoted to defining slang used by young people) demonstrates the backlash. Here is the top definition under the entry "Black Jesus":

> Well, it's true. Sorry, KKK and the like. Did you really expect Me to be lily-white in a region like the Middle East? Hellooo… Jews are Semitic? I looked more like an Arab or Egyptian than I did like George Bush.**

The author (who goes by the handle "Black Jesus") cannot be assumed to represent any particular demographic. This is just one person's voice. Even so, notice that he or she attempts to convey the obvious fact of Jesus's geography and assumed physicality by casting any detractors as white supremacists. In a more measured tone, video blogger Franchesca Ramsey attempts to correct the pop culture assumption in her MTV News video:

---

* Blum, E.J. and Harvey, P., *The Color of Christ: The Son of God and the Saga of Race in America* (Chapel Hill: The University of North Carolina Press, 2012), p. 13.
** "Black Jesus," *Urban Dictionary*. [Online]. (URL https://www.urban-dictionary.com/define.php?term=black%20jesus). (Accessed March 29, 2018).

While a Korean or a black Jesus might not be historically accurate –
just like a blond-haired, blue-eyed Jesus – people of color have the
right to see themselves in their religion, especially after centuries of
being taught and forced to worship a God that doesn't look like them.*

In this case, we see a conscious creativity motivated by social
awareness. Black Jesus is not a corrective to white depictions
of Jesus; rather, the corrective is to the previously unchecked
assumptions of racial hierarchy.

Jesus and sports culture

The film *Major League* (1989) is a comedic look at baseball culture. The key characters in this story are fictional baseball players
who exhibit an array of stereotyped personalities. Some players
are superstitious, some are antisocial, and some are hedonistic. The
film also includes a window into Jesus worship in America. In
one scene, the power-hitting Cerrano says: "Jesus, I like him very
much; but he no help with curveball." His Jesus-loving teammate
replies: "You trying to say Jesus Christ can't hit a curveball?" These
characters are, of course, caricatures but a conversation like this
may well take place in any baseball locker room and in America
especially.

Professional athletes must navigate "office politics" that
include Jesus. In this way, sports are not unlike other professions.
Teammates host Bible studies and prayer meetings. Prayer sometime takes place on the field as a public show of faith, and some
players use their media platforms to bring attention to Jesus. For
example, after winning the Women's World Cup, US midfielder

---

* As quoted from "What Did Jesus REALLY Look Like? | Decoded,"
MTV News; December 16, 2015. [Online]. (URL https://www.youtube.
com/watch?v=mPRnrfTHeL4). (Accessed March 29, 2018).

Lauren Holiday explained: "The wonderful, wonderful thing about loving Jesus is, it's not about me. And the spotlight isn't on me. So when I do step out on the field, I get to play with freedom because I don't have to worry about if I score or what happens if we lose or if I make a bad pass, because success isn't determined on that with Christ."*

As the quotation from *Major League* suggests, Jesus is sometimes appealed to as an important factor in performance. This can take the form of kissing a cross-shaped necklace before or after a play. Another example would be focused and meditative quiet as one's regular routine. Prayer to Jesus can also be an important part of dealing with on-the-field failure or major injury.**

In New York in 1951, no rivalry was more important to baseball fans than the Giants vs. the Dodgers. In a match that would decide which team would advance to the World Series, Bobby Thomson (Giant) hit a game-winning home run against pitcher Ralph Branca (Dodger). Thomson's success brought the Giants a 5–4 victory. So unlikely and emotionally charged was the game that it became known as the "Miracle of Coogan's Bluff." After the game, Branca left the ballpark devastated. He spoke to the Reverend Pat Rowley, a Catholic (Jesuit) priest, who tried to console him. Branca asked the priest, "Why me?" Rowley

---

* Ashcraft, M. and Ellis, M., "Christian soccer players bring home Women's World Cup: a profile of Lauren Holiday," *God Reports*, July 9, 2015. [Online]. (URL http://blog.godreports.com/2015/07/christian-soccer-players-bring-home-womens-world-cup-a-profile-of-lauren-holiday/). (Accessed March 29, 2018).
** Examples of such testimonies are distributed by a Christian parachurch organization called Athletes in Action. See Balmer, R.H., *Encyclopedia of Evangelicalism* (2nd edn; Waco: Baylor University Press, 2004), p. 42.

Figure 30 Tebowing: Former University of Florida quarterback, Tim Tebow, is pictured kneeling in prayer (January 1, 2012). Tebow's love for Jesus became a popular topic during his short and mediocre career as a professional athlete. In addition to praying in public, he would sometimes paint "John 3:16" on his face as an evangelistic effort.

answered: "Ralph, God chose you because he knew you'd be strong enough to bear this cross."*

---

* Goldstein, R., "Ralph Branca, Who Gave Up 'Shot Heard Round the World,' Dies at 90," *New York Times*, November 3, 2016. [Online]. Retrieved from https://www.nytimes.com/2016/11/23/sports/baseball/ralph-branca-who-gave-up-shot-heard-round-the-world-dies-at-90.html

The priest's advice is indicative of the popular Christian belief that God uses emotional hardship as a teaching tool. In suffering, Christians live in the pattern of Christ who suffered on the cross. Christian athletes will sometimes use this rationale as way to alleviate worry. Conversely, it is quite common for Christian athletes to publicly thank Jesus when they succeed. Jesus, then, is involved in both victory and defeat.

Elton John's gay Jesus

In *Parade* magazine (2010), the British singer and songwriter Elton John gave an interview, saying: "I think Jesus was a compassionate, super-intelligent gay man who understood human problems." In addition to being a Rock and Roll Hall of Fame inductee, Elton John is a philanthropist and a long-time advocate for the gay, lesbian, bisexual, and transgender community. He has often spoken publicly of his life as a gay man, husband, and father. Speaking of Jesus, he said: "On the cross, he forgave the people who crucified him. Jesus wanted us to be loving and forgiving. I don't know what makes people so cruel."

ABC News sought a response from Bill Donohue, the Catholic League president. Donohue chided Elton John, saying that "to call Jesus a homosexual is to label Him a sexual deviant." Reverend Sharon Ferguson demurs in response to John's claim:

"I don't think that comments like this are particularly helpful," Reverend Sharon Ferguson from the Lesbian and Gay Christian Movement told ABC News.

"He challenged our understanding of loving one another in his relationship with his disciples and friends, so we should be taking on board the total inclusivity of Christ when it comes to the notion of sexual identity and orientation but that does not mean that we should make any assumptions about Christ's sexual activity or lack of it." Whatever the fallout, it puts the Rocket Man firmly in the eye of a storm of controversy, once again. The magazine is out on newsstands Saturday.*

There are at least four agendas at work in this news piece. Elton John's agenda seems to include advocacy for a group that has historically been persecuted. Bill Donohue's agenda seems to include a defense of a more traditional view of sexual normalcy. Sharon Ferguson seems to value reconciliation between an often exclusive Church, and a historically persecuted group. Finally, both *Parade* magazine and ABC News seem to be publicizing this controversy to sell a product. The commonality among all four is that the name "Jesus" is wielded to advance an agenda. For better or worse, Jesus's name is an ideological force. This has been true in Christendom for two millennia, and is no less true now.

This, of course, is just one narrow window into a much larger debate about sexuality and gender in the Christianized West. It is quite common for Jesus's name to be dropped into such conversations. In my own experience, I most often hear advocates for gay equality remind us what Jesus did *not* say. For example, former US President Jimmy Carter said: "Homosexuality was well known in the ancient world, well before Christ was born, and Jesus never said a word about homosexuality."** But claims such

---

* Gallego, S., "Elton John: Jesus 'Super-Intelligent Gay Man,'" ABC News, 19 February 2010. [Online]. Retrieved from http://abcnews. go.com/Entertainment/elton-john-jesus-super-intelligent-gay-man/ story?id=9889098
** Raushenbush, P.B., "President Jimmy Carter Authors New Bible Book, Answers Hard Biblical Questions," *Huffington Post*, March 19, 2012. [Online]. Retrieved from http://www.huffingtonpost.com/2012/03/19/ president-jimmy- carter-bible-book_n_1349570.html

as Elton John's, that Jesus was gay, though a relatively new talking point, are increasingly common.*

It is worth noting, however, that this debate often assumes a simplistic understanding of gender. Either Jesus is gay or straight. It is a move away from the binary construct of male vs. female, but it is just substituting one binary for another. A better question is this: Jesus calls himself a "man" in the gospels, but what sort of masculinity did Jesus represent?**

American Christianity: Oh-yeah-and-Jesus-too-I-guess

American Christianity is changing. Americans are generally less attached to doctrine, Bible reading, and historic Christian ethics. Because of this, American notions of Jesus are evolving too.***

The National Study of Youth and Religion is a sociological study of 3,000 young people and their parents that offers a big-picture look at the religious lives of American teenagers (2001, 2009, and 2015). Authors Christian Smith and Melinda Lundquist Denton sum up the current American approach to religion as "Moralistic Therapeutic Deism." But what Smith and Denton found is that young people tend to believe that "God is something like a combination Divine Butler and Cosmic Therapist: he is always on call, takes care of any problems that arise, professionally

---

* It should be pointed out, however, that this notion was once entertained by Christopher Marlowe (1564–93) in literary circles.
** I address this question in my book *The Wife of Jesus: Ancient Texts and Modern Scandals* (London: Oneworld, 2013).
*** This cultural shift may be indicative of more global trends too. I focus, here, on my own culture to provide a snapshot of one segment of Jesus in pop culture.

helps his people to feel better about themselves, and does not become too personally involved in the process."*

While Moralistic Therapeutic Deism (MTD) was originally meant to label a particular generation of American teenagers, it probably indicates a larger trend among Americans. Christian Smith and Patricia Snell followed up this study by surveying "emerging adult" participants in 2009.** Kenda Creasy Dean suggests that the youth surveyed most likely reflect the faith of their parents.*** Moreover, MTD is now a multigenerational trend that probably extends well beyond American culture.

In sum, many Americans believe that a divine Creator exists, but only gets involved with human affairs when a problem is especially vexing. This Creator wants people to feel good, be nice, and get along with each other. Good people go to heaven after death. These are general beliefs rather than a concrete life ethic or creed. While MTD bears little resemblance to historic Christianity, many of those surveyed consider themselves Christian. As such, Jesus was also mentioned – albeit vaguely and reluctantly – in many of the National Study of Youth interviews.

Many of the people surveyed "were comfortable talking generally about God but not specifically about Jesus."**** The study revealed a common ambivalence about Jesus, even among those who attended church. They expressed belief in God and Jesus, but this belief didn't influence their lives outside church. "A number

---

* Smith, C. and Lundquist Denton, M., *Soul Searching: The Religious and Spiritual Lives of American Teenagers* (Oxford: Oxford University Press, 2005), p. 165.
** Smith, C. and Snell, P., *Souls in Transition: The Religious and Spiritual Lives of Emerging Adults* (Oxford: Oxford University Press, 2009).
*** Creasy Dean, K., *Almost Christian: What the Faith of Our Teenagers is Telling the American Church* (Oxford: Oxford University Press, 2010).
**** Smith and Lundquist Denton, *Soul Searching*, p. 267.

of Christian teenagers we interviewed conveyed an 'Oh-yeah-and-Jesus-too-I-guess' kind of attitude in trying to express their core religious beliefs."*

America, of course, is still mostly composed by those who consider themselves Christian and who have traditional, religious notions about Jesus. In their 2009 book, *Souls in Transition*, Smith and Snell summarize:

> About two out of three emerging adults (68 percent) claim to believe that Jesus was the son of God who was raised from the dead. Eleven percent says Jesus was an important human teacher but not the son of God. And 1 percent says Jesus never existed.**

Importantly, those who have been labeled "Moralistic Therapeutic Deists" in this sociological study would not use that label themselves. Indeed, at least 68 percent echo historic Christian doctrine when asked directly about Jesus (even if they are reluctant to talk about it). That said, the *Oh-yeah-and-Jesus-too-I-guess* attitude marks an important element of the Christian experience. Jesus may be a well-known point of doctrine, but knowledge of his life and teaching is scant among many Christians. Most importantly, religious allegiance to Jesus has very little influence on the way that Americans live.

Jesus memes

Memes, in the world of social media, combine short phrases and images that encapsulate an idea. The pithy idea can be humorous, political, derisive, or inspirational. The word "meme" was first coined by Richard Dawkins to be a more general phenomenon:

---

* Smith and Denton, *Soul Searching*, p. 135.
** Smith and Snell, *Souls in Transition*, p. 121.

We need a name for the new replicator, a noun that conveys the idea of a unit of cultural transmission, or a unit of *imitation*. 'Mimeme' comes from a suitable Greek root, but I want a monosyllable that sounds a bit like 'gene'. I hope my classicist friends will forgive me if I abbreviate mimeme to *meme*. If it is any consolation, it could alternatively be thought of as being related to 'memory', or to the French word *même*. It should be pronounced to rhyme with 'cream'.*

The internet meme, then, attempts to create an imitable unit of pop culture to convey an idea.

I tend to encounter Jesus memes on Facebook. Perhaps due to my selection of "friends," I most often encounter Jesus

Figure 31 Conservative Jesus (circa twenty-first century).

---

* Dawkins, R., *The Selfish Gene* (2nd edn; Oxford: Oxford University Press, 1990), p. 192.

memes as political statements. For example, I often see a variation of the following: Jesus stands before 5,000 hungry people
(cf. Mark 6:31–44) in conversation with one of his disciples.

This meme creates a double irony: Jesus, who famously fed
the hungry and commanded his followers to do the same, is now
pictured as a crass politician. He refuses to feed hungry people due to his fiscally conservative ideology. In this way, Jesus
becomes a caricature. The second underlying irony is that (generally speaking) American Republicans tend to boast a greater
devotion to Jesus, yet their political policies seem to betray the
belief that poor people are a burden to taxpayers.

A similar meme uses the same image with the following caption: "Verily I say unto you; every one of these moochers is get-
ting drug tested before they eat! (Republican Jesus)." Again we
see the same irony. From this progressive point of view, the meme
"Republican Jesus" is an oxymoron.

Now consider this meme from the opposite point of view.
Using the same image, Jesus is pictured as saying, "I told you
to feed the poor, not create laws that steal from people to do
it!" The caption reads: "Libertarian Jesus." This meme projects
a fiscally conservative voice onto Jesus, but not as a caricature.
Jesus, in this case, positively embodies the values of conservatives. This meme makes the point that many Christians are
quite generous, but they don't trust taxation as a means to live
by Jesus's ethics.

In both cases, Jesus is co-opted to serve a political agenda. In
American politics, competing ideologies tend to use Jesus as an
advocate for both sides. Both proponents and protestors of capital
punishment use sayings of Jesus to make their points. We see the
same dual portrait along the lines of sexuality debates. The invention of the internet meme is just a new way to create Jesus in our
own images.

Homeless Jesus

The Canadian figurative artist Timothy Schmalz invites us to meet the real Jesus again in his interactive sculpture titled *Homeless Jesus*. The original life-sized piece was set along the sidewalk at Regis College, University of Toronto (2013). Replicas have been installed in several other major cities around the globe while other pieces have been installed at the Vatican.

Figure 32 *Homeless Jesus* (2013): Pictured here is a replica installed in San Antonio, Texas.

Homeless Jesus became infamous, however, once it was installed outside St Alban's Episcopal Church in Davidson, North Carolina. Residents near St Alban's mistook the sculpture for a living, breathing "vagrant," and called the police to have the offender removed.

Schmalz brings together several levels of aesthetic realism. On the face of this faceless portrait, Jesus is realistic; he is real enough to be mistaken for a real person. This leads us to ask the question: *If homelessness wasn't a real problem in the first place, would anyone have called the police to have "Jesus" removed?*

The only marks that distinguish this statue as Jesus are the nail wounds in both feet. But notice also that there is enough room on the bench to sit at his feet. Thus Schmalz's Jesus invites encounter and participation. Jesus becomes real on a fourth level as he is tactile.

But not every person in Davidson appreciated the invitation. One neighbor to St Alban's Episcopal found the sculpture off-putting: "Jesus is not a vagrant. Jesus is not a helpless person who needs our help."*

In a way, this criticism falls in line with one element of Christian orthodoxy. Christians commemorate and worship a risen Christ. The Book of Revelation progresses from the por-trayal of Jesus as a slain lamb to a victorious warrior. But even in these post-Easter reflections we see the image of a kingly judge who instructs: "Come, you that are blessed by my Father, inherit the kingdom prepared for you from the foundation of the world; for I was hungry and you gave me food, I was thirsty and you gave me something to drink, I was a stranger and you welcomed me, I was naked and you gave me clothing, I was sick and you took care of me, I was in prison and you visited me." (Matt. 25:34–6)

Christians throughout the ages have created sacred space and time to encounter the forsaken Jesus. This is what the offended neighbor misses in her rush to censor Schmalz's sculpture and

---

* Quoted from video, "Homeless Jesus statue sparking debate," CNN Belief Blog, February 28, 2014. [Online]. (URL http://religion.blogs.cnn.com/2014/02/28/homeless-jesus-statue-sparking-debate/). (Accessed March 29, 2018).

Figure 33 *Homeless Jesus* (close-up): Author's own photograph of the pierced feet. (Thanks to Timothy Schmalz for permission.)

thus "clean up" the neighborhood. Additionally, it is noteworthy that neighbors were only fooled by the statue when observing it from a distance. Those who sat at Jesus's feet experienced the art differently.

Jesus and refugees

Over the course of this book, we have seen that Jesus – for artists, historians, politicians, etc. – tends to reflect the assumptions and ideals of contemporary culture. It is therefore understandable to be suspicious when an anti-Semite argues that Jesus somehow destroyed Judaism (see earlier: Renan). Doubt is warranted when a warlike people portray Jesus as a great warrior (see earlier: The

Heliand poem, p. 130). We should question Eurocentric artists who paint Jesus with pale skin and blue eyes.

Keep in mind, however, that not every ideological assumption or ideal is misleading. For example, Martin Luther King, Jr., emphasized that Jesus taught his followers to be non-violent. This emphasis clearly builds from King's ideology but it doesn't change the fact that Jesus did indeed teach non-violence, and that his earliest followers seem to have taken this to heart. So while King's portrayal of Jesus clearly reflects his own ideals, it just so happens that King was correct.* Consider, then, the following reflection on the Christmas story by President Barack Obama in 2016:

> As we retell the story of weary travelers, a star, shepherds, and the Magi, I hope that we also focus ourselves on the message that this child brought to this earth some 2,000 years ago. A message that says we have to be our brother's keepers, our sister's keepers. That we have to reach out to each other, to forgive each other, to let the light of our good deeds shine for all. To care for the sick, and the hungry, and the downtrodden. And of course, to love one another, even our enemies, and treat one another the way we would want to be treated ourselves. It's a message that grounds not just my family's Christian faith, but that of Jewish Americans, Muslim Americans; nonbelievers and Americans of all backgrounds. It's a message of unity and decency and a message of hope that never goes out of style.**

---

* It is important to note, however, that Jesus's teaching about non-violence should not be confused with modern pacifism. These ideologies overlap, but they are not exactly the same.

** "Remarks by the President at Lighting of the National Christmas Tree," Office of the Press Secretary, December 1, 2016. [Online]. (URL https://obamawhitehouse.archives.gov/the-press-office/2016/12/03/remarks-president-lighting-national-christmas-tree) (Accessed March 29, 2018).

Obama used the story of Jesus's birth as a call to "unity and decency" at a time of great division in America. Many Christians feared their Muslim neighbors and rejected Muslim refugees as a result. No doubt, Obama's political agenda is reflected in his retelling of the Christmas story. Here again, Jesus conveniently mirrors the politics of the politician, but that does not make Obama's interpretation faulty.

Historian Joan Taylor, responding to a rejection of refugees in the United Kingdom in 2016, sought to remind people about Jesus's own refugee status:

> In the Gospel of Matthew, Jesus's (adoptive) father Joseph and mother Mary live in Bethlehem, a town in Judaea near Jerusalem. It is assumed to be their home village. Certain *magoi* ('wise men'/ astrologers) come from 'the East' to Herod, the Roman client king of Judaea, looking to honour a new ruler they have determined by a 'star', and Jesus is identified as the one. All this is bad news to Herod, and Herod acts in a pre-emptive strike against the people of Bethlehem and its environs. He kills all boys under two years of age in an atrocity that is traditionally known as 'the massacre of the innocents' (Matthew 2.16–18). But Joseph has been warned beforehand in a dream of Herod's intentions to kill little Jesus, and the family flees to Egypt. It is not until Herod is dead that Joseph and Mary dare return, and then they avoid Judaea: Joseph 'was afraid to go there' (Matthew 2.22) because Herod's son is in charge. Instead they find a new place of refuge, in Nazareth of Galilee, far from Bethlehem. Jesus's earliest years were then, according to the Gospel of Matthew, spent as a refugee in a foreign land, and then as a displaced person in a village a long way from his family's original home.*

---

* Taylor, J.E. "Jesus was a Refugee," The Jesus Blog, September 7, 2015. [Online]. (URL http://historicaljesusresearch.blogspot.com/2015/09/jesus-was-refugee.html). (Accessed March 29, 2018).

Taylor acknowledges that many historians will label this story as historical fiction; but she does not read this account as wholesale fiction. After all, Herod was known for his paranoia and severe reactions to those who represented a threat to his power. Moreover, the general Jewish experience at that time involved political displacement and refugee status, often in Egypt. She goes on to suggest that this experience may well have informed Jesus's ethics:

> The legacy of being a refugee and a newcomer to a place far from home is something that I think informed Jesus's teaching. When he set off on his mission, he took up the life of a displaced person with 'nowhere to lay his head' (Matthew 8.20; Luke 9.58). He asked those who acted for him to go out without a bag or a change of clothing, essentially to walk along the road like destitute refugees who had suddenly fled, relying on the generosity and hospitality of ordinary people whose villages they entered (Mark 6.8–11; Matthew 10.9–11; Luke 9.3). It was the villagers' welcome or not to such poor wanderers that showed what side they were on: 'And if any place will not receive you and refuse to hear you, shake off the dust on your feet when you leave, for a testimony to them' (Mark 6.11).*

Taylor concludes by pointing readers to the Red Cross Europe Refugee Crisis Appeal. In this way, she hopes that her readers will help present-day refugees who face a similar plight as Jesus's family. It would be safe, therefore, to say that Taylor's politics correspond to her portrait of Jesus.

The cases of Obama and Taylor present a more complicated form of the "mirror" effect discussed in this book. It is, after all, possible that the ethics of a politician or historian reflect a close and critical reading of the gospels. So our simplistic and knee-jerk suspicion of a mirrored portrait will not do. Indeed, this is where the metaphor of a mirror becomes inadequate. At times (as

---

* Taylor, "Jesus was a Refugee."

we see in the example of Jesus as a refugee) the artist, historian, politician, etc., has been impacted by Jesus and has been transformed by this impact. We should expect, in such cases, that they will project their transformative encounter back onto to their portrait of Jesus. Instead of a simple mirror, we might imagine the scenario created by two mirrors facing each other.

Conclusion

Pop-culture images of Jesus can be profound, funny, and both at the same time. They can be observant, absurd, or both. But they are not benign. Pop-culture portraits betray the flaws, limits, and agendas of those who create them. They can also impact those who consume them unwittingly.

My hope is for athletes who invoke the name of Jesus to be better aware of the problems created by their words, however well intentioned. I hope readers of this book will learn to challenge the pervasive whiteness of Jesus in the Western imagination. I also hope that progressive readers will acknowledge the historical setting of Jesus's teachings – i.e. not every progressive cause will be supported by Jesus's words. Most importantly, I would urge readers to seek out Jesus's views on the topics he addressed directly. Social justice, the danger of being preoccupied with security, and the reality of evil are examples of topics that Jesus dealt with directly. If, indeed, we continue to use Jesus's legacy in modern dialogues, we should be willing to be challenged by his words.

Jesus's pop-culture presence must be tempered by some awareness of Jesus's historical personality, and some self-awareness about our propensity to co-opt Jesus for our own interests.

Five books about Jesus and pop culture

Blum, E.J. and Harvey, P. *The Color of Christ: The Son of God and the Saga of Race in America*. (Chapel Hill: The University of North Carolina Press, 2012).

Crossley, J.G. *Jesus in an Age of Neoliberalism: Quests, Scholarship and Ideology*. (Reprint edn; New York: Routledge, 2014).

Detweiler C. and Taylor, B. *A Matrix of Meanings: Finding God in Pop Culture*. (Grand Rapids: Baker Academic, 2003).

Prothero, S. *American Jesus: How the Son of God Became a National Icon*. (Reprint edn; New York: Farrar, Straus and Giroux, 2004).

Reinhartz, A. *Jesus of Hollywood*. (Oxford: Oxford University Press, 2009).

Concluding reflection

Over the course of this book, we have seen that artists, philoso-phers, historians, and religious folk tend to use Jesus as a mirror. Portraits of Jesus often reflect the cultural assumptions or ideals of the time and place in which they are painted. This tendency is true of devoted followers of Jesus and critical historians alike. It can be seen in Renaissance sculptures and in the latest memes. This mirror is at work in voices of dissent that hate tradition, as much as in the most pious hymns.

But knowing that the mirror effect is inevitable can help us. When we look for Jesus and see too much of ourselves in him, it is possible to begin the process of self-critique. I approach Jesus as a historian. I approach the evolution of Jesus's portraiture like an observer of cultural trends. In both ways, I am suspicious of my interpretation when it does not challenge me. Occasionally I dis-cover something of our common humanity in Jesus's words. But, ultimately, Jesus is not convenient. He will not automatically back up my political leanings or justify my pop-culture consumption. The mirror effect can – if we allow it – become a tool for self-critique and self-awareness. It may not be possible to be objective when we study Jesus in history, literature, religion, scholarship, and culture. But it is possible to be honest with ourselves as we make the attempt.

Jesus will continue to serve as a cultural cipher. His legacy has attracted the biases and agendas of disparate communities, and will continue to do so. Jesus will be used to justify both misogyny and feminism, just as the Bible was used to justify both slavery and abolitionism in previous generations. Jesus will be cast as a voice of the oppressed and a prop for the oppressor. In short, his legacy is as malleable as the Western imagination. But Jesus is not – indeed, should not be – an empty container. Students of history can – if they are honest – be self-aware. We can pause to reflect on our cultural biases and political agendas. We can reject portraits of an anti-Semitic or pro-capitalist Jesus as inappropriate uses of his legacy. We can also reject notions of a modern, progressive Jesus who fits too easily within our post-Enlightenment narratives.

We can still encounter Jesus as a prophetic voice if we are willing to participate with an open mind and an open heart.

Subject index

References index